# HOLA MISS

## MELLIE NAPOLITANO

New Degree Press

Copyright © 2020 Mellie Napolitano
*All rights reserved.*

HOLA MISS

ISBN    978-1-64137-541-2   *Paperback*

978-1-64137-542-9   *Kindle Ebook*

978-1-64137-543-6   *Digital Ebook*

*To those seeking acceptance.*

# CONTENTS

———

*"People mistakenly assume that their thinking is done by their head; it is actually done by the heart which first dictates the conclusion, then commands the head to provide the reasoning that will defend it."*

—ANTHONY DE MELLO

# INTRODUCTION

———

I stood talking on the phone outside of Washington Elementary, a public school in a low- to middle-income neighborhood of Washington, D.C. In my role as a community support worker for a nonprofit organization called Grace House, I worked with families at the school, connecting them with basic resources including food, shelter, health services, and legal aid. I told my mom over the phone, "I'm going to start doing house visits with my clients." My mom, possibly taking my call from our six-bedroom house in a historic neighborhood of Atlanta, knew this meant going to the homes of Latino immigrants, many of whom were undocumented.

There was a pause on the other end of the phone. "I'm not sure if I like you doing house visits, Mellie. Is that safe?"

The anger welled up inside of me. *What do you mean, is that safe?! Who and what are you listening to on the news? I* thought. "Mom," I said. "This is important to me. My clients need help. They would never do anything to hurt me."

"I'm your mother, Mellie," she said. "Can't I just be concerned for your safety?"

*NO!* shouted the twenty-three-year-old, self-righteous side of me. *No, you can't, Mom! Not if it means making me feel that you don't understand what my clients are going through. They would never hurt me!*

But if I was so sure that they would never hurt me, then why did I hesitate when approaching one of my clients' apartment buildings on a house visit? Why did I think to myself, *Well, it's a sunny day. Some cars are going by, so I don't think anything will happen to me.* I thought these things because, like my mom, I had heard the stories about immigrants: they're violent and bring crime and drugs into the country.

I don't remember having any strong convictions about immigration prior to my work with immigrants. Besides, when it came to politics and policy, I just accepted the mainstream conservative viewpoint on it.

Working with Latino immigrants put me in a position to see that the rhetoric around immigrants is often false and leads to misconstrued policy. I grew up in a politically conservative family, and I still maintain many conservative values. However, as a result of my work, I have a liberal view on immigration. This is a book about my time working with immigrants and what I learned as a result of my experience.

\* \* \*

My mom and I were not alone in our misinformed beliefs about immigrants and crime. A Gallup poll shows that 42 percent of Americans believe that immigrants are making the crime situation worse in the United States.[1] Meanwhile, an article from the Cato Institute says, "All immigrants have a lower criminal incarceration rate [than citizens] and there are lower crime rates in the neighborhoods where they live, according to the near-unanimous findings of the peer-reviewed evidence."[2] The data shows the disconnect between commonly held beliefs and reality.

The immigrants I worked with came to the United States because their countries were riddled with poverty, violence, and corruption. They went to school, worked one or more jobs, and wanted to learn English. But political candidates and representatives often vilify immigrants as job-stealing, drug-dealing criminals. In the same speech that Donald Trump announced he was officially running for president, he said, "When Mexico sends its people, they're not sending their best. ... They're sending people that have lots of problems. ... They're bringing drugs. They're bringing crime. They're rapists. And some, I assume, are good people."[3] Based on my experience of working with immigrants, I don't agree with the image of immigrants that Trump depicted in this speech, or with similar rhetoric that I've heard from other candidates and representatives.[4]

1    "In Depth: Topics A to Z: Immigration," *Gallup*, 2020.

2    Alex Nowraseth, "Illegal Immigrants and Crime—Assessing the Evidence," *Cato Institute*, March 4, 2019.

3    "Transcript: Donald Trump Announces His Presidential Candidacy," *CBS News*, June 16, 2015.

4    Johnny Kauffman, "Georgia Candidate for Governor Doesn't Plan to Use 'Deportation Bus' to Deport Anyone," *NPR*, May 16, 2018.

While Trump called out Mexican immigrants in this specific speech, more immigrants are now returning to Mexico than entering into the U.S. The Mexican economy has improved and there are now more jobs in Mexico.[5] Most Latino immigrants now come from Central American countries, including Guatemala, El Salvador, and Honduras, and they are fleeing because their home countries are plagued by poverty and violence—which the U.S. played a role in perpetuating.[6] However, when they seek refuge in the U.S., we tell them that they can't stay here either.[7]

To understand immigration in the U.S., it is crucial to separate fact from fiction. By sharing my story of working with immigrants, I hope to put a human face on the immigration issue. The point of my book is not to give a list of policy recommendations but rather to emphasize a person-focused framework for thinking about immigrants and immigration. The same way that my personal encounters with immigrants forced me to question my own beliefs, I hope this book will expand readers' thinking on the issue and lead them to ask themselves what they believe about immigrants and why they hold those beliefs. May my book foster a discussion about treating others with compassion—regardless of their legal status.

5    Michelle Mark, "More People Are Moving From the US to Mexico than the Other Way Around," *Business Insider*, May 30, 2019.

6    Daniel Gonzalez, "The 2019 Migrant Surge is Unlike Any We've Seen Before. This Is Why," *USA Today*, September 25, 2019; David Gonzalez, "In Today's Headlines, Echoes of Central America's Proxy Wars of the 1980s," *The New York Times*, February 27, 2019.

7    "Asylum Decisions and Denials Jump in 2018," *TRAC Immigration*, November 29, 2018.

\* \* \*

As a political conservative (who voted for Trump in 2016), I am in a unique position to write about this topic. I'm not writing about my pro-immigrant stance because of my party allegiances. Instead, I am doing so because of my encounter with immigrants.

I went to Georgetown University for college, and while I was there, I learned Spanish and spent much of my time working in D.C. as a volunteer for a literacy program called "Reading Road." After, graduation, my experiences as a tutor and Spanish-speaking skills led me to seek positions in schools, during which I often worked with Latino immigrants. I continued to work with Latino immigrants in D.C. for two years, first as a sports coach and then at the aforementioned nonprofit, Grace House.

One of my clients at Grace House, Mario, left El Salvador and crossed the southwest border by himself. He was sixteen years old and was a thoughtful, hard-working student. One day, while meeting in my cramped office, he said, "Miss, my friend Diaz needs your help."

"Okay," I said. "I'll reach out to him." I met with Diaz in my office a few days later. He was seventeen and had also emigrated from El Salvador. His long brunette hair covered most of his eyes, and he was so quiet that it was hard for me to hear him speak. "Would you like to talk to my colleague, Sarah?" I said. "She's a therapist and it might be helpful to talk with her about some of the experiences you've had of immigrating here."

"Okay," he agreed.

I made the referral and touched base with Sarah after their meeting. "How did it go?" I asked.

"He's been through a lot," she said. "He watched his best friend get killed in his front yard before he left his country."

That first meeting was the only time that Sarah met with Diaz. She tried to meet with him again, but he wasn't in his classes when she looked for him, and he never stopped by her office on his own. Since then, I met with him several other times and gave him information about places he could get food and health resources. I wanted to do more for him, but I didn't know how to do it. I hope that by sharing my story, I *can* do more for him.

* * *

Every day, I drive home from work on a stretch of road in Atlanta named Buford Highway. This road runs through a community that is home to thousands of immigrant families. Although it is one of the most heavily foot-trafficked roads and busiest public bus routes in the city, many parts of the street have no sidewalk, leading to multiple pedestrian deaths every year.[8] I see men, women, and children who look like my former clients at Grace House walk down the dirt path alongside the road. They wait for the bus in the 95-degree heat or pouring

---

8    Angie Schmitt, "The Campaign to Fix Atlanta's Most Dangerous Street and Preserve Its Immigrant Cultures," *StreetsBlog USA*, September 21, 2017.

rain. I sit in my air-conditioned car and change lanes to pass the bus. But there's a small voice inside me saying, *"Serve them."*

A friend once told me that a lot of the time, that small voice inside of us is God. *So here I go, God.*

This book is for conservatives and people who are politically centrist or liberal with conservative friends or relatives (because we have to talk to each other about things like immigration to reach a compromise!). I understand that a conservative may be skeptical of a pro-immigration argument—I felt the same way before I worked with immigrants. I aim to share what I learned through my clients, and this knowledge is grounded in facts about immigration on a national scale.

A few notes before I proceed: I have changed names in my book for privacy reasons. In cases in which I do not specify whether an individual was documented or undocumented, it is either because I wasn't aware of their legal status at the time or including their status was not essential to the story. While documented and undocumented immigrants face distinct barriers based on their status—and I call out some of those differences in my book—there are many barriers that they do share. I want to draw attention to those commonalities through their stories.

Next, countless data sources exhibit immigrants' positive contributions to the U.S.—from economic, social, and healthcare perspectives, to name a few.[9] I have chosen to

---

9    Gretchen Frazee, "4 Myths About How Immigrants Affect the U.S. Economy," *PBS News Hour*, November 2, 2018; Nunn, Ryan, Jimmy

largely leave out those facts because they are secondary to the purpose of my book, which is to show how immigrants are valuable because of who they are (human beings), and not because of what they've done or what they can do for the U.S. Finally, this is *my* story about my encounter with immigrants, told from *my* perspective. While I aim to do my clients and neighbors justice in my descriptions of their stories, I trust that they would share their stories and perspectives in ways that are distinct from my own.

In my book, I share stories about real people facing real challenges, including the story of my client, Sonia, who cared for her undocumented brother who was in a coma; the story of my client, Camila, who waited for her teenage children to cross the border and reunite with her and her three-year-old child in D.C.; and my own story of how working with immigrants changed my views about immigrants and immigration. *Hola Miss* is the story of how my encounter with immigrants changed *me*. I hope that by reading my story, you will see how a new perspective on immigration might change *you*.

---

O'Donnell and Jay Shambaugh, "A Dozen Facts About Immigration," *Brookings*, October 9, 2018.

# CHAPTER ONE

# FAMILY

---

I grew up in an affluent, conservative family in Atlanta, Georgia. I adopted my parents' conservative political values, as well as their religious and social values. When my oldest sister, Caroline, started going to school, it became clear to my parents that she would thrive in a smaller classroom setting. They thoroughly researched their options and tried a few different schools, but none of them were right for her. Ultimately, my mom felt God calling her to create a Christian school for Caroline and other students with learning differences.

When I was six years old, my mom, with my dad's support, created Sophia Academy and admitted the first class of eleven students. The school logo was a square of four thumbprints above the words "No Two Are Alike." The experience of watching my parents value my sister and her education so much that they would create a school for her taught me many lessons. It taught me that rather than seeing differences as shortcomings, we should see them as assets. It taught me the importance of serving individuals on the margins of society. Most of all, it instilled in me that every child—every person—is valuable. Balanced with my conservative political values, it was this value of treating people fairly that I carried with me into young adulthood and the start of my professional career.

\* \* \*

In the spring of 2014, I graduated from Georgetown University in Washington, D.C. While studying there, I worked for a student-run consulting organization that provided pro bono services to nonprofit organizations. I liked the consulting experience. Plus, after attending one of the most expensive universities in the country, I felt pressured to prove myself by landing a high-paying job at a well-known company. Consulting and banking jobs were the most popular and sought-after jobs at Georgetown. I spent a good chunk of my senior year applying for positions with consulting and banking companies, but all of them rejected me.

I reflected more on my next steps and thought about how, during college, I had been involved in a tutoring program in D.C. called "Reading Road." A few times a week, we drove to the Northeast edge of the district to tutor elementary school students in some of the poorest neighborhoods in the city. Most of these schools were located in what's called a "food desert," meaning that there's no fresh produce located within a few miles. Many of the houses lining the school resembled the shotgun-style house that Martin Luther King's family lived in in Atlanta. Being there, I felt like this part of the country hadn't experienced the Civil Rights Movement yet because the vast majority of the residents were African American, and the area lacked the grocery stores, updated textbooks, retail stores, and extracurricular activities that were available in the parts of D.C. that were populated by more white people.[10]

Reading Road taught me about the education gap and its ties to racial and income inequality. Studies show that, across the U.S., students living in poorer districts have access to fewer educational resources and opportunities than students living in more affluent areas.[11] The student body of the school that I tutored in was 99 percent African American and all of the students qualified for the federal free lunch program. The reading level of the students fell below national standards and that of their peers who attended the Georgetown public schools.

I tutored one student, Isaiah, for two years. After months of working together, Isaiah still preferred to read the book *No No, Yes Yes* by Leslie Patricelli (which only contained those words) over and over again. I would look out the window and daydream during the forty-minute drive to his school with the other tutors sharing the van. *Maybe today Isaiah will want to read a different book,* I thought. *Maybe today, he'll show signs of progress.*

On the way home, we would debrief as a group. "Well, Isaiah had a rough day today," I shared with the group. "Thank you, Mia," I said to our coordinator, "for helping me get him out from under the table." Mia would give me ideas to try the next time, and I would try them all, but most of the time they didn't work.

---

10    "2019 Demographics," *DC Health Matters*, January 2019.

11    Alana Semuels, "Good School, Rich School; Bad School, Poor School," *The Atlantic*, August 25, 2016.

One afternoon, I tried to engage Isaiah by doing a reading exercise with him in the hallway. The school custodial worker walked by and saw that Isaiah wasn't answering my questions. "Isaiah," he said. "Stop acting up." Isaiah looked up at him and didn't say anything. The man then led him into a hallway closet.

I stood outside the hallway, frozen. *What is going on in there??? What do I do?!* I didn't hear anything.

A few moments later, the custodian stepped back out, and Isaiah stepped out from behind him. The man informed me that Isaiah's mom had given him permission to "rough him up" if the boy acted out.

The man left, and it was just me and Isaiah in the hallway. I knelt down next to him. "Isaiah," I said. "Did he do anything to you?" He didn't answer me, but a tear rolled down his cheek.

I reported the incident to our program director when I got back to the Reading Road office. When my class schedule changed, I kept tabs on Isaiah through his new tutor. I was glad that he continued working with Reading Road, but the thought of Isaiah's school and home life haunted me.

I wanted to help Isaiah by fixing his school. Looking back on this now, I realize that I was naive to think that I could, or should, fix his school on my own. I disagreed with his mom permitting the school custodian to "rough him up," but I thought, *I can't change his mom. The school is the answer. If his school could just be better, his life would be better. He would have more opportunities.* Because of Isaiah and students like him, I shifted my focus after graduation to an end goal of a career in education policy, but first I wanted to work on the ground level in schools. *If I work on the ground level,* I thought, *then I'll see the issues firsthand and I'll learn how to fix them.*

\* \* \*

I applied to various jobs in schools and got an AmeriCorps position with GameDay, a national nonprofit organization. In this role, I led kindergarten through fifth grade students in sports and games at Washington Elementary, which was located in a low- to middle-income neighborhood in D.C. largely populated by African American and Latino immigrant families. I stuck out. I was one of very few white, blue-eyed, blonde-haired people walking around the school.

I wasn't sure if my parents knew what I was doing on a day-to-day basis at GameDay, but I felt pretty certain that they didn't understand why I was doing it.

At a party, a family friend asked my mom what I was up to. My mom responded, "Mellie's coaching basketball to students in D.C."

The friend asked, "Does Mellie know how to coach basketball?"

My mom apparently responded, "We don't know."

Not only was I a Georgetown grad who had just taken a coaching job on an AmeriCorps stipend, but I also didn't have any experience as an athlete. I was involved in theater in high school. At GameDay, I was teaching kids how to play sports that I didn't play myself, and the job didn't even have the clout of a program like "Teach for America." I had achieved my goal of being on the ground level, figuratively, literally, and psychologically.

I had conflicting feelings about my achievement. At times, I felt confident that my firsthand experience would pay off down the road when I got into education policy. But at other times, the doubt would creep in and I would feel that I was wasting my time on a job that didn't have a clear upward trajectory. Sometimes, I felt ashamed that I had taken a lower-paying job than most of my peers from Georgetown, but I was also proud of myself for taking the road less traveled and pursuing a job where I was serving others.

It's comforting that my mom knew *what* I was doing at GameDay, even if she didn't know *how* I was doing it. We did receive training on how to coach the sport, by the way. My 5'3" stature coupled with my basketball inexperience didn't lend itself to being a basketball pro, but I think the girls on the team had a fun time.

Coach Mike, whose child was one of my players, volunteered to be the assistant coach. Coach Mike had more basketball experience than I did since he had played in high school and still played pickup occasionally with his friends. He was African American, probably in his thirties, and wore black athletic shorts, socks, and sneakers—usually with a whistle around his neck during practices. Before he became my assistant coach, I had noticed him and his wife dropping their kids off at school together in the morning. They had four daughters, one still in a stroller. He was excited to be the assistant basketball coach and hoped that one day his daughter, Destiny, would go to college on a basketball scholarship. He taught the girls to shout "Money!!" (pronounced Mon-ay) when they shot their free throws. It was nice to have him around at practices because he gave more substance to the team and made the girls laugh.

Soon, Coach Mike's background check came back with some criminal activity, and my manager told me that he couldn't be my assistant coach anymore. I was sad to lose him and planned out how I would tell Coach Mike. I brought him to the side at school the next time that I saw him. I told him, "You've been such a big help, and the girls and I have loved having you as an assistant coach ..." feeling awkward and scratching the back of my neck nervously, "... but your criminal background check didn't pass—so, unfortunately, you can't be the official assistant coach anymore." Coach Mike's face held the same deer-in-headlights look the entire time I spoke; afterwards, he exhaled, nodded, and said, "Okay. Can I still come to the games?" I assured him that yes, of course he could, and he smiled softly and thanked me. At most games, he was among other parents in the bleachers, watching Destiny play. I think we won one or two games that season.

∗ ∗ ∗

While I had taken the GameDay job as a means of learning about schools and how to "fix" the education system, through experiences like the one with Coach Mike, I realized that some problems were systemic: they were bigger than the school. In Coach Mike's case, his criminal record prevented him from being a volunteer coach. In many families' cases, poverty held students back from achievement. One report says, "In general, schools that serve students from higher-income families educate significantly higher-achieving students than schools that serve high concentrations of students in poverty."[12] My interest in education policy began to wane as I realized that there was no easy fix to these greater societal issues.

While speaking with some of the students' parents at Washington, I thought to myself, *How can I expect these parents to prioritize education when they're worried about paying their rent or putting food on the table?* Many of the families I worked with faced so much poverty that their capacities to nurture their children's education were very different from my parents'. Besides the difference in income levels, my mom helped us with our homework, and we ate dinner as a family most nights. On the other hand, some of my students were in foster care, and they would only see their parents on scheduled dates. Other students didn't see their parents at dinnertime because their parents worked two jobs.

Throughout the years that I volunteered and worked in the D.C. school system, all of the schools where I worked provided free lunch to the entire student body based on the student demographics. At my job that followed Gameday, I would see many similarities in the systemic barriers faced by both low-income Americans and Latino immigrant communities.

---

12    Amy Hegedus, Ed.D, "Evaluating the Relationships Between Poverty and School Performance," *NWEA*, October 2018.

Not having found any solutions during my time at GameDay that I could apply to a career in education policy, I started thinking about other career options. My parents had said for years that I would be a good lawyer, so when my now-husband, Paul, started studying for the Law School Admission Test (LSAT), so did I.

Saint Augustine of Hippo said, "Peace in society depends upon peace in the family." At the same time that I was seeing the importance of the family unit in the school and community in which I coached, I was also feeling pressure from my own parents to follow a more traditional line of work. It was easier to follow their dreams for me than to figure out what my dream for myself was.

"I'm going to apply to law school," I told my parents.

"Really?!" they asked in tandem on speaker phone. "That is so exciting, good for you!! Are you going to take a test prep course? We'll help you out if you need some money!"

It felt so good to be doing something that my parents were excited about. The small voice inside me kept waving a red flag and asking, *Are you sure about this?* But I ignored it. It felt better to make my parents happy and go with the clear path of applying to and attending law school than to let them down and figure out the big, *Then what are you going to do now?* question.

In the meantime, I was nearing the end of my ten-month Americorps commitment as a GameDay sports coach, and my mixed feelings about the job had morphed into a resolute dislike. I didn't feel mentally stimulated in the job, and I was ready to never play dodgeball again. For weeks, I blasted a particular pop song on my headphones during the ten-minute walk from my house to work. In the song, the artist sings about praying at the river. I would listen and pray, *Please, God. Help me be patient with the kids. And please, God, help me find a new job.*

My AmeriCorps commitment ended, and I retired as Coach Mel. Still, I felt compelled by the immigrant families in the community where I lived and worked to do something. Based on my interactions with students and my conversations with Washington Elementary teachers and social workers, I saw that many immigrant families there lacked access to community resources. I knew my ability to speak Spanish would help me work with the families, and I found immigration and community-based work interesting and stimulating. I didn't want to be in the education field, but I still wanted to be "on the ground" in the community, to see where I fit in and how I could make a meaningful contribution. I job-searched while I studied for the Law School Admission Test (LSAT).

Soon, I was invited to interview for the position of bilingual community support worker at Grace House. Grace House is a nonprofit organization that provides medical, social, and educational services to individuals in D.C. and Maryland. As a community support worker, I would help clients access basic resources including food, shelter, career services, and education.

The interview started off well. Two managers from the mental health team interviewed me. I was nervous and waited for them to test my Spanish. *I can do this, I can do this, I can do this,* I told myself. Even though I minored in Spanish in college, I had doubts about whether my Spanish was good enough for everyday communication. But the language test never came, and I got the job. *You'll do fine with the Spanish,* I told myself. *Direct immersion is the best way to get better at the language, anyways.* I didn't know it at the time, but direct immersion would not only improve my Spanish—it would also force me to question my stance on immigration and see immigrants in a way that I never had before.

## CHAPTER TWO

# WORTHY

———

On my first day at Grace House, the director of our team took me out to lunch. Ours was the school-based mental health team, and it was made up of about fifteen therapists (many of whom were bilingual) and one other bilingual community support worker besides me.

"I'm so excited about the position and to be part of the team," I gushed. "I'm excited to hear what schools I'll be at."

The director looked surprised. "Oh, HR didn't tell you? You're going to be at Washington Elementary and Central High."

This was the best news I could have received about my school assignments. I had worked at Washington Elementary the previous year as a GameDay sports coach, and Central High was a high school a few blocks away. *I can't wait!* I thought. Over the next few days, I binge-watched Spanish YouTube videos and practiced my Spanish with my now-husband, Paul.

I knew that my new role would be challenging, but I didn't expect to feel unworthy of my job a lot of the time. Some of my feeling of failure resulted from being new and inexperienced. Some of it was because of my environment. And some of it was due to the barriers that my clients faced.

In my role as a community support worker, I met with clients one-on-one and referred them to organizations and agencies that provided resources, such as food, career services, medical care, and mental health services. I also provided "therapy lite" interventions and personal development strategies, including positive coping mechanisms as well as organizational and time-management skills. The goal of my position was to help clients function at optimal levels despite mental health issues or barriers to social services.

Sarah, an older and more experienced Grace House therapist, had begun working at Central High the year before. The first day that I arrived at Central, Sarah showed me my workspace. She explained, "The principal said that we could share an office … which isn't going to work." Instead, she had spoken with the Central social workers, and they had decided I could use the common area with a desk outside their offices to meet with clients.

Sarah gave me one of my first referrals at the high school. The student's name was Diego. "He needs health insurance," she said. She introduced us in Spanish saying, "Miss Mellie will be helping you apply for medical insurance."

"Hola Miss" (pronounced 'Mees'), he said, smiling. I chose to go by "Miss Mellie" since using my last name seemed too formal. Like Diego, most of my clients just called me "Miss"—I wasn't sure if that was because they forgot my name, or because it was just easier to say "Miss."

Diego was skinny, had short, brown, gelled hair, and was a few years younger than me. We sat down and I started explaining the pages-long health insurance application to him. He looked confused, which made me doubt myself. *It's my Spanish*, I thought. *He can't understand me.* Feeling nervous about my Spanish, I laughed. Then he laughed. This happened a few more times as I explained the application. Sarah peered around her office door and gave us a look. My stomach lurched. *Oh no, she thinks we're flirting.* I returned to reviewing the form, and finally we reached the end of it.

"Okay," I said. "Do you think you and your uncle will be able to go in person soon to submit your application?"

"Si, gracias, Miss."

*You say yes, but you kind of look like you mean no*, I thought. He seemed confused about the process, and I wasn't convinced that he would make the trip soon. *It's my fault*, I thought. *He didn't understand what I was saying.*

When meetings with several other students went the way that Diego's went, I asked Sarah if I could rehearse the health insurance application dialogue with her. She agreed to help me, and I ran through the form with her. When I finished, I looked up, afraid and embarrassed that she might tell me that my Spanish needed a lot of work. To my surprise she said, "That was great." She gave me a few pointers on local jargon for terms like "check" and "rent" but said that, otherwise, I explained it all very well. After rehearsing it with Sarah, I figured that my Spanish-speaking clients were giving me blank stares because the application was long and confusing, regardless of language.

* * *

Paper shortages were an issue for me at Central because paper was not kept in or near the printer. Staff were expected to keep it in their offices. Since I didn't have an office, I kept printer paper, a few copies of the health insurance application, and other forms and lists for my clients in my backpack.

One day, I prepared to meet with a client. I needed to print out some resources, so I reached into my bag for printer paper, but to my dismay, there was none there. *Oh no*, I thought. Sarah was in her office meeting with a client for a therapy session. This was a problem because the social workers at Central were not very nice to me. They didn't seem to want me there, and I felt like I was a nuisance to them. The three of them had worked at Central for several years, and they were in their thirties and forties. They only spoke English, so they served the English-speaking students, while Sarah and I and another external staff member served the Spanish-speaking students. When they introduced themselves to me as "Mrs. Austin" and "Ms. Daniel," I knew that their intention was not that we would be friends. I would be their subordinate.

I didn't know when I would see my client next, and I needed to print the document, so I got up and knocked on one of the social workers' open doors. "Excuse me. Hi, Mrs. Austin. I'm sorry—can I have a piece of paper?" Mrs. Austin looked up at me. She took a long pause before she reached into her drawer. Then she stood up and handed me two pieces of paper. "Here you go," she said and closed her door in my face.

A few weeks later Sarah told me, "I have good news: you're getting your own office." The bad news was that my move was the result of my client meetings disturbing the other social workers. I'm not sure what their expectation had been when they assigned the first space to me. Maybe they thought I wasn't going to interact much with clients. Regardless, I picked up my bags and walked down the hallway with Sarah, where she showed me my new space near other faculty offices.

My new office locale wasn't much more welcoming than the old one, and I didn't have Sarah near me anymore either. I felt so awkward sometimes, like an impostor in that office. Students would come around the corner to my new office, and I would perk up—thinking that they were coming to speak to me. "Mr. Sanchez?" they would ask, and I would point them to Mr. Sanchez's office.

My isolation at Central was partly my fault. I could have spoken more to the staff members whose offices were near mine or brought baked goods to bribe them to be my friends. But the few times I did speak with them, they barely raised their eyes from their work to look at me. It seemed like they had no interest in who I was or why I was there.

One day, there was an assembly and the principal pulled an employee onto the stage who worked for El Centro, a non-profit organization at the school. She was a native Spanish speaker and recent Harvard graduate, and at Central, she helped coordinate extracurricular activities for the students. The principal spoke into the microphone and doted on her, saying, "This intelligent young woman is a Harvard grad, working with our students this year through El Centro." The principal went on about how great the woman was.

My lower self spoke up inside: *Huh. What about me?* My higher self responded, *Well, it's nice that she's here, and that she's working with the students.* My lower self said, *But you, Mellie? You're worthless.*

\*\*\*

Even though I often felt isolated and unworthy of my Grace House job, there were moments that made me want to persevere and keep going. At Central, I witnessed up to forty students at a time attend my colleague Sarah's support group for immigrant students who had experienced trauma. While it was sad that so many students had a need for the support group, I was encouraged by the strides Sarah had made to remove the stigma around mental health. For example, many students came to her office to meet with her on their own accord, and her clients often recommended that their friends see her too.

Once, I presented to Sarah's support group about my services and how I could help them access health care, health insurance, clothes, and food. I was nervous because it was one of the first times that I presented to a group of people in Spanish. I was twenty-three at the time—and some of the students were eighteen and nineteen—so I felt like I was presenting to a group of my peers. I was aware of how much I didn't know or understand about their experiences. So many of them had walked through the desert and crossed the southwest border alone after facing gang violence and poverty in their home countries. I had never experienced anything like that growing up in Atlanta.

During my presentation, the young men and women looked at me with curious looks on their faces. I thought, *They're probably wondering what I'm saying because my Spanish isn't very good. They probably don't trust me because I'm white and I'm not like them. I'm not an immigrant. I'm not Latina.*

Parts of my inner dialogue were true: I am not an immigrant, and I am not Latina. But there were parts of it that were not true. We did have certain things in common: we all could have been called outsiders at Central based on the fact that D.C. wasn't our home, and we didn't have wide networks at the school. I, like the immigrant students, struggled with language: they struggled with English, and I struggled with Spanish. And like some of the students in the support group had shared with me in one-on-one sessions, I wanted so badly to feel accepted. Even though at times I felt unqualified for the job, I cared so much about it and about my clients. I wanted to hear their stories and help connect them with resources. I wanted to tell them, "I value you," and I wanted them to value me.

I finished the presentation, and there was a moment of silence. Thinking that I had probably bombed the presentation, I wanted to say "Adios" and walk out the door. But then they started clapping for me, and many of them broke into smiles. Relieved, I smiled too. When they clapped for me, I felt accepted. They had faced sadness and denigration an unknown number of times in their countries and in the U.S. as part of their stories of immigration. I stood in front of them that day speaking to them in their own language, telling them I wanted to work with them, and they accepted me.

*  *  *

During moments like these, I felt worthy of my job. One Saturday morning, my friend, Mary, and I were getting out of D.C. for the day to go hiking. Mary picked me up, and we drove northwest toward Great Falls, Maryland. I pointed out Central High as we drove by, and the next thing I knew— BAM! a car on the opposite side of the street hit a biker. The biker flipped over his bike and landed on the ground. From my quick glance at the biker, I thought it might be a Central student. Mary and I both gasped, and time froze for a moment. The question *What should we do?* floated without words in the air.

"Can you turn around?" I asked Mary. "That might be one of my students." *I'm sure Mary thinks I'm trying to be a hero right now,* whispered my lower self. *Go ahead then! Go help him!* whispered my higher self.

"Yeah, yeah, of course." Mary said. She put on her blinker. "Um …" she said, looking for a place to turn around. She turned the corner and headed back in the direction we came from.

We parked on the corner, got out of the car and walked over to the biker, where the driver and a few bystanders had gathered and were making sure he was okay. He was Latino and wore a black hoodie and jeans. He sat on the sidewalk and looked more shaken up than hurt. The color had drained from his face, and his hands were scratched up. His bike lay on the ground next to him.

"Hi," I said, and I told him I worked for Grace House at Central. He looked up at me, squinted, and then his eyes relaxed.

"I recognize you," he said. "I've seen you at the school." *He recognizes me,* I thought. *He knows who I am.*

The EMTs showed up a few minutes later and brought the student into the ambulance. I asked him if I could do anything to help him. He told me that he had been on his way to work. He gave me his boss's number and asked me to call his boss to tell him he wouldn't make it to his shift. Once I did that, I asked him what else I could do.

"Can you keep my bike until I can get it back from you?" he asked.

"Of course," I said, and Mary and I spent the next few minutes trying to jostle it into the trunk of her car. *Darn it, go in you darn bike, the kid didn't ask for much—just go in the car.*

But then I noticed the student climbing back out of the ambulance and coming over to me and Mary. "I'm not going to go the hospital, I'm okay," he said.

"Are you sure?" I asked. *Are you not going because you're okay, or because of something else?* I thought, but I didn't ask. If he had said he didn't want to go because of financial or legal reasons, I didn't know what I would say or do next. He assured us that he was in good enough shape to go home, so he dislodged his bike from the car and started walking it back in the direction he came from.

Mary and I walked back to the car. "I'm glad he's okay," she said.

"Me too, that was scary," I agreed. I felt worthy of my job that day, not because I did the right thing, although that did make me feel good. I felt worthy because the student recognized me and accepted my help.

It was hard working at Grace House because even though I intended to do a good job, sometimes I felt like I was totally failing. It felt like I was the problem—I thought, *I'm too white,* or *I'm too young,* or *My Spanish isn't good enough.* But when the student noticed me, those insecurities fell away. He noticed me, and he saw me as someone he could allow to help him, and it didn't feel like there was something wrong with me anymore. In that moment, when his eyes relaxed and he let me help him, I felt like I was in exactly the right place. I felt worthy.

## CHAPTER THREE

# DREAMS

---

Oftentimes, when I looked for my client, Diego, in his classes at Central High, I couldn't find him. At one of our meetings, I asked him about this. "Where were you the other day?" I asked. "I didn't see you in your English class."

"Miss," (pronounced Mees) he said. "School is hard. My English is really bad. I don't understand the teachers. It's hard for me to get up in the morning. Sometimes, I don't want to get out of bed."

"It's okay, Diego," I said. "Your English will get better. You have to come to school, though." I felt a kinship with Diego. Often, I felt like a foreigner while working for Grace House myself; out of place, out of my element. I didn't look like anyone else or seem to have a similar background to anyone else. I could understand why Diego didn't want to come to school sometimes.

As I mentioned earlier, Diego was first referred to me to get D.C. health insurance, which all D.C. residents qualified for regardless of citizenship status. When I learned that he had an attendance issue at school, I started working with him on time management and goal setting. I showed him how to make to-do lists and set alarms on his phone. I provided therapy lite interventions, such as motivational interviewing and positive coping mechanisms.

One morning, I spotted Diego in the cafeteria. He was facing the other direction, and I started walking over to him, but he seemed to know I was there and turned around before I could tap him on the shoulder.

"Hi, Miss," he said. He told me he was very proud of himself that morning for arriving before school started.

"That's wonderful, Diego!" I told him. It was gratifying to see him make positive changes and get excited about them. I was sad when Diego told me he and his family were moving to Maryland before the school year ended. I would miss his familiar face around the school.

"I don't want to go, Miss," he told me. "I won't make friends."

"Diego," I said, "do you have friends here at Central?"

"Yes," he answered.

"How did you make them?" I asked.

He recounted the ways. I asked him if he could do it again, and he replied, "Yes, Miss."

I wasn't worried about Diego making friends. I knew he would endear himself to others at his new school. He wrote me a note before he left. "Miss Mellie," he wrote. (*Score!* I thought. *He does know my name!* Since so many of my clients called me "Miss," it was refreshing to hear Diego use my name.) "You helped me to feel like I had value, and that you have to dream and fight for your dreams for them to become a reality... You helped me realize that in life you will always face hard times, but you should never stop fighting for your dreams."

In moments like these, I felt like I was helping my clients work toward and achieve their goals.

\* \* \*

I built my client base from teenage students at Central High and parents of students at Washington Elementary—which were about a mile apart from each other. If work got slow at Washington, I rode my bike to Central hoping to meet with more clients there. Central's cafeteria was my least favorite place to look for a student. With only a few years of age separating me from my clients, and as one of the only blonde-haired, white women, I got many curious looks from students. *Just walk straight ahead and pretend you know exactly what you're doing,* I told myself.

But I often struggled to build my client base, probably due to many factors. Adult clients worked one or more jobs, so scheduling meetings with them was difficult. It took me a few months to build rapport with staff who might send me referrals. Gaining my clients' trust took time too. A few referrals hung up on me when I called them to offer support services. I have to think that the fear of deportation made my clients hesitant to work with me, as clients often asked me and my colleagues whether working with us would affect their status.

In fact, many community organizations see that undocumented immigrants don't seek services because they fear the risk of deportation.[13] My colleagues and I had reason to believe that working with us would not affect their status, so we always told them not to worry about that. However, recent initiatives to penalize recipients of public benefits threaten to make this fear a reality.[14] It makes me sad to think that some immigrant parents won't apply their citizen children for food and health benefits because they're afraid of being deported, but I can understand their decision.

I imagine that my clients felt a similar isolation to me. My high school clients were away from their home countries and families, didn't speak much English, and were trying to learn U.S. History from the ROTC coach while sending money back home to their families in El Salvador or Guatemala. I couldn't wrap my arms around the obstacles they faced, and I felt a general wistfulness about how to help them.

Once, our director told our school-based mental health team, "It's helpful to use analogies with clients to understand how

---

13    Katie J. Ducklow, "Lessons for Social Workers: A Review of the Latino/a Undocumented Immigrant Experience," *Sophia*, the St. Catherine University Repository Website, 2017.

14    Sarah Holder, "How Rule Changes About Public Benefits Could Affect Immigrants," *CityLab*, August 13, 2019.

they're feeling. For example, if they feel lonely and they don't know how to get help—'It sounds like you feel like you're in the middle of the ocean in a raft without a paddle.'" *How did she just come up with that?* I thought. *And how do you say paddle in Spanish?*

Well, it felt like my clients and I were like reeds being tossed by the wind in the desert. We had somehow ended up at Central, and it was a lonely, barren place.

*\* \* \**

It was in this environment that, to my surprise, I found that I shared similar dreams and aspirations as some of my clients. Alfredo was one of them. He was a high school student at Central, around eighteen or nineteen years old. He always flashed a big smile and gelled his hair. He had a soccer player-type physique, walked with a swagger, and spoke some English. I wasn't sure where his parents lived, as Alfredo told me he lived with a friend. He came to school most days and had an entrepreneurial spirit—he sold some health, beauty, and home care products on the side.

I taught Alfredo how to make a vision board because I could tell he was an optimistic, goal-oriented person, but I also knew that he had an issue with attendance. "Going to school will help you accomplish your goals," I said. "Google things that you want to do and see, and we'll print them out and put them all together to make a vision board."

He smiled a big toothy smile and started googling. He put a picture of the Barcelona soccer stadium on his board and a man at a podium giving a talk to an arena filled with people. He pointed to the picture of the speaker. "This is what I want to do, Miss," he said.

"What's that?" I asked.

"I want to be a successful businessman and talk to thousands of people about business," he replied. Under the picture of the speaker, there was a picture of the Eiffel Tower.

*Wow,* I thought. *I have a picture of Spain on my vision board. I have a picture of Paris on my vision board too. But how is Alfredo going to get to either of those places? I don't think he has an American passport or any money to travel. But I'm not going ask him* how *he'll do it. If this is what he really wants, he'll find a way.* "This is wonderful, Alfredo." I said. "You can do all of these things. Do you see how school could help you accomplish these goals?"

"Yes," he said, and we discussed the benefits of a high school degree, and why it was important to come to school on time.

Similarly, I explained to my client, Henry, another high school student, how to make a vision board. I learned that Henry had a wife and a baby. "I want to take care of them, Miss. I want to be a truck driver," he said.

*You want to be a truck driver?* I thought. *It's not my dream, but I won't stop you from going after yours.* I googled, "Can undocumented immigrants get a driver's license in D.C.?" I found that they can get a restricted license, but I struggled to figure out whether that license would qualify for truck driving.[15] Maybe I was projecting my own framework for success onto Henry because what I ended up saying was, "I'm having trouble finding information about this. In the meantime, can we focus on getting your high school degree and the skills you need to do well in your classes?"

"Okay, Miss," he said, and we changed gears.

\* \* \*

Afterward, I went home to my Craigslist group house and climbed the stairs to my windowless room. I sat down on the bed and looked up at my own vision board next to my bed. On it, there was a picture of my family and a picture of Paul's family. There was a Parisian scene, a picture of Madrid, and pictures of Atlanta, Michigan (where Paul's family lives), and D.C. *How is this all going to work?* I wondered. *What am I doing?*

Similar to my clients, I didn't know how I was going to achieve my goals and I didn't see how my present reality fit into the bigger picture of my life. Unlike my clients though, as an American—not to mention a white American from an affluent family—there were no glaring systemic barriers standing between me and my goals. I believed that my clients could achieve anything that they set their minds to, but I wanted to stand up and shout from the mountaintops, *Why does it have to be so much harder for some people? Why is it*

---

15  "States (And D.C.) That Allow Driver's Licenses for People in the Country Illegally," *Procon.Org*, December 20, 2019.

*easier for me just because of my skin color, the country I was born in, and the parents that I was born to? WHY?*

I knew the answer to my question was a history of policies and events interwoven with prejudice, racism, and classism—all of the things that propped me up and kept my clients held down. I had been, and sometimes still am, guilty of these things myself. But noticing the similarities between me and my clients made me want to take away the barriers that divided us. It made me want other people to see the similarities too because I was learning that I couldn't take down those barriers on my own.

## CHAPTER FOUR

# FRIENDS

---

I sat with friends at lunch one day. Sam, my friend who used to work in admissions at a competitive state university, lamented the monotony of college application essays: "Oh, the number of kids who talk about how a mission trip changed their lives …"

"Oh yeah," my friend, Ashley, agreed. Her boyfriend, Mark, had worked in admissions at the same university. "Mark told me about that. It's just the same story over and over again."

"I wrote about a mission trip on my college essay," I said. Ashley looked at me and tried to give me an out. "I'm sure yours was nuanced, though—not like the others."

"No, I don't think so," I said. Honesty is one of my best and worst qualities. "I'm pretty sure I just talked about how it changed my life." There was an awkward silence and someone changed the subject.

I remembered that trip and specifically that day at the dump in Nicaragua. The smell of rotten food and burning trash came back to me ...

I walked hesitantly through the dump, which was swarming with flies. I was a high school junior on a mission trip with an organization called "Friends and Familia" (usually just "Friends" for short). People foraged through the dump in bare feet, collecting tin cans and other reusable materials that they could give to the government waste collection in exchange for money. These people lived in the dump and bathed in the greenish-black water that flowed through it.

Before the "tour" of the dump, the director of Friends and Familia provided some background on the community who lived there. When Hurricane Mitch caused a mudslide to hit the already impoverished country in 1998, the Nicaraguan government moved the displaced individuals to the dump with the promise that it was a temporary solution.[16] However, over a decade later, the government had not yet made good on that promise.

Friends staff would go into the dump community and explain their mission: that they would work alongside the Nicaraguans to help them build homes on land outside the dump. "We tell the Nicaraguans," the director said, "we'll work with you and your neighbors to build homes in another part of town. But you have to do the work too, and no one can move into their house until all of the neighbors'

16    History.com Editors, "Hurricane Mitch," *History, A&E Television Networks*, Updated November 11, 2019.

homes are built." *Huh, I thought. That's an interesting way to do things.* "Some people don't take us up on our offer," explained the director. "They are afraid to leave the dump. They know what to expect there." *That's sad, I thought. I guess I'm not that surprised, though. People, myself included, are afraid of change.* Besides the fear of change, I'm sure that there were other reasons for their decision to stay at the dump, but as a high school student, this particular reason stood out to me.

During my mission, Friends staff—along with Nicaraguans in the community—dug holes and laid water pipes so that they would have access to clean water. Friends and Familia could have afforded the heavy machinery needed to dig the holes, but they chose to dig with shovels instead. They made this choice to maintain their mission of working alongside the people, building lasting relationships, and making their community's growth sustainable. Friends changed the way that I think about foreign (or domestic) aid. It also provided a backdrop to my understanding of U.S. involvement in Central America particularly during the 1980s and 1990s.

In the 80s, a proxy war (a war instigated by a major power which does not itself become involved) between the Sandinistas and the U.S.-backed Contras embroiled the country in civil war.[17] This civil war continued the streak of poverty that Nicaragua was already experiencing due to natural

---

17    *Lexico Dictionaries* s.v. "proxy war," accessed February 4, 2020; David Gonzalez, "In Today's Headlines, Echoes of Central America's Proxy Wars of the 1980s," *The New York Times*, February 27, 2019.

disaster and corruption.[18] Similar proxy wars involving the U.S. occurred in other Central American countries, leading to increased poverty and unrest.[19] None of my Grace House clients were from Nicaragua, but it made me sad to hear them describe the similarities between their home countries and what I saw on my mission trip. It made me even sadder to know that many of my clients didn't have legal status and, therefore, their ability to stay in the U.S. was unknown.

Friends leadership, when talking about their mission, said, "Before you go in and help someone, even if you think you know what that person needs and what's best for them, you have to ask them what they need—they have to be part of that conversation." They explained, "The person in need often knows the fastest and most innovative way to meet their needs because they know their needs better than anyone else." Asking that question was a guiding principle for the Friends team. As a result, they now build modern bathrooms and provide microloans to entrepreneurs in their communities, and they've seen community-driven success with projects like these. Working with Friends made me wonder what U.S. diplomatic affairs would look like if we asked our counterparts, "What do you need?"

---

18    Rocha, Jose Luis, Thelma Martinez and Ximena Rocha, "Summing Up Hurricane Mitch: The Good, the Bad and the Ugly," *Envio*, December 1999.

19    David Gonzalez, "In Today's Headlines, Echoes of Central America's Proxy Wars of the 1980s," *The New York Times*, February 27, 2019.

* * *

I told Paul about my lunch conversation with my friends
and he laughed. "Mellie, why did you out yourself like that?"
"Because it's true," I said. "Working with Friends and Familia
did change my life. I wanted to speak up for myself and for
other people who had similar experiences." Paul responded,
"I've read articles about the sort of thing your friends were
talking about." He showed me an article that poked fun at
people who came back from mission trips and changed their
Facebook profile pictures to a picture of them from the trip.
I remembered putting up a similar profile picture of myself.
"Welp, I did that, too," I said.

People can make fun of me for it, but I'm grateful for the
perspective that the mission trip gave me. Now, when I think
about "sending immigrants back home," I know what "home"
might look like. And I understand why an immigrant would
risk staying here without documentation rather than going
back home.

## CHAPTER FIVE

# LIFE

———

"Carmen's in her second trimester," my Grace House colleague, Sarah, told me as she gave me a new referral. "Her mother hasn't spoken to her since she found out she was pregnant. She needs help making sure she has prenatal care and resources for her baby." *But I don't know anything about babies!* I panicked inwardly. Outwardly, I nodded my head, not wanting my colleague to know that I was freaking out. *If I tell Sarah I don't even know where to start, she will think I'm incompetent and may not give me any more referrals,* I thought. "Okay," I said in a voice I hoped sounded calm.

"Carmen." I wrote in my notebook. Next to it I wrote, "Pregnant. Needs help."

In the doom and gloom side of my brain, these words were in ALL CAPS, had five exclamation points *!!!!!* next to them, and an emoji of a wide-eyed face with the head popping off. However, by refusing to write the words in this way, the all-positive side of my brain was trying to encourage me: *It will be okay, Mellie. You can do this. You can help Carmen, a pregnant teenager who's estranged from her parents and has no rights* *or money, prepare to bring life into the world.* I'm pro-life, but I wasn't thinking about the fact that Carmen had chosen life when she was first referred to me. It scared me that she was pregnant and that I was supposed to be able to help her. I didn't know that over the next few weeks, as a result of working with Carmen and another pregnant student named Luisa, I would have a crash course in pregnancy and preparing for a child.

Luisa and Carmen were two of my first clients, both referred to me by Sarah, a therapist on our school-based mental health team. Both Luisa and Carmen were Spanish-speaking immigrants and expecting babies within the next few months. They needed information about labor and delivery, resources for their babies, and information about returning to school after the birth of their children. Even though I'm pro-life, I'm not sure if I ever said "congratulations" to either client. I was twenty-three at the time and I was overwhelmed by the idea that these young students, a few years younger than myself, were pregnant. I couldn't imagine what they were going through and what they would go through once they had their babies, and I felt bad that being pregnant had curtailed their own adolescence. Instead of becoming a statistics wiz or soccer star, their main focus was now prenatal appointments and preparing for their babies.

I set about connecting them with resources. First, I arranged for each client to meet with the in-school pregnancy resource coordinator at Central. This resource for young parents was available in eleven of the twenty-one D.C. public high schools. Before the first meeting, the coordinator listed some of the available resources like diapers and bottles, and added, "We have breast pumps if they want them; the Latina moms often breastfeed." I was glad that the coordinator insisted on using a translation service because I had never seen a breast pump myself, and I didn't know how to say "breastfeed" or breast pump" in Spanish. The switched-off overhead lights and stacks of diapers, wipes, and other baby supplies that lined the walls of the coordinator's office emphasized the feeling that the walls were closing in on me. I wanted to get my pregnant clients out of their current situations—but didn't see an escape route.

One day, I walked into Carmen's classroom to pull her out for a session. She was very pregnant, around five feet tall—a few inches shorter than me—and asleep at her desk. Carmen's teacher called her name, and she woke up and met me in the hallway.

"Hola, Carmen," I said.

"Hola, Miss," (pronounced "Mees") she said quietly, with a soft smile and heavy eyes.

"Como estas?"

"Cansada," (meaning tired), she said.

During our meeting that day, I explained that the school allowed a six-to-eight-week maternity leave, depending on the type of delivery. She nodded and didn't ask many questions.

Luisa, on the other hand, just seemed annoyed every time I met with her. She seemed like someone who was used to taking care of herself and didn't like asking for help. Whenever I asked her, "Is there anything else you need help with," she would always say a quick, "No, I'm fine," and head for the door. Her toughness made it hard for me to work with her, but I was less worried about her than sweet, quiet Carmen.

Now that I'm a mom—and since I took twelve weeks of maternity leave after my son, James, was born—it's hard for me to imagine going back to school in half that time. Plus, I had a lot of family to help me, which wasn't the case for either of my clients. I would call Carmen and Luisa weeks after the six-week mark to ask them if they were coming back to school. Carmen's voice was still quiet and Luisa still sounded annoyed. There were often noises in the background and when I asked how their babies were doing, both of their voices took on a more tender tone. "Muy bien," they said. After a few months, I would see them every few weeks or so at school.

There weren't any outwardly pregnant students at the high school I attended, and the differences between my high school and Central reflected the national numbers. Teenage pregnancy is more common among Latina women than most racial groups in the U.S. The birth rate for Hispanic teens was 28.9 per 1,000 women in 2017 versus the national average of 18.8.[20] Moreover, pregnancy rates increase as income decreases; studies show that adolescents living in low-income neighborhoods with less job opportunities have higher rates

20  "About Teen Pregnancy," *Division of Reproductive Health, National Center for Chronic Disease Prevention and Health Promotion,* March 1, 2019.

of pregnancy than their peers living in high-income neighborhoods with more job opportunities.[21]

The coordinator of the young parents' organization shared with me that there were several other pregnant students besides Carmen and Luisa at Central at that time. None of my friends or siblings had babies, so in my meetings with Luisa or Carmen, I often felt like I didn't have much of a foundation to stand on and I didn't know what to say to my clients. I felt helpless and unqualified for the job. I prayed for the right words and resources to comfort and help Luisa and Carmen.

At the time, my now-husband, Paul, and I attended St. Monica's, a Catholic church in D.C. We were Sunday school teachers there and knew some of the church staff. One of the staff members put me in contact with a woman named Teresa who worked for a Catholic-based pregnancy aid center called Haven of Peace. When I told her about my clients, the first thing she said was, "Thank God they decided to keep the babies."

Hearing those words was like a light bulb for me. Teresa reminded me of something that I believed but had lost sight of, and for the first time, I saw Carmen and Luisa's pregnancies as gifts rather than curses. I saw that Carmen and Luisa had made a choice to keep their babies. I had been so wound up in the doom and gloom part of them being pregnant teenagers that I failed to see the beauty of their choices to be

---

21   "Trends in Teen Pregnancy and Childbearing," *Office of Population Affairs, U.S. Department of Health and Human Services*, Accessed January 23, 2020.

mothers. That change in perspective gave me hope that Luisa and Carmen and their babies would be okay. I saw that the situation was bigger than me or my clients—in a good way.

I shared the Haven of Peace resources with my clients, but I'm not sure if they ever contacted Teresa or Haven of Peace. Neither Luisa nor Carmen came back to school consistently after having their babies, but they both returned at least intermittently. When they did come back, they came back changed. They came back as mothers. While I recognized during their pregnancies the huge responsibility that they were about to take on, I failed to understand how their children would be blessings to them. When Luisa and Carmen returned to school, I saw how strong they were. I saw their courage to face their peers as teenage moms and the stigma that comes with it. I saw their determination to continue learning in their classes. I saw women who often stayed at home to take care of their children.

\* \* \*

While I haven't come across anyone who has argued that immigrants aren't human, anti-immigration groups often talk about immigrants in a dehumanizing way. President Trump, as the leader of the US, has described immigrants as murderers, rapists, illegals, and aliens.[22] At the same time that Teresa reminded me that my clients had chosen life, my work with immigrants taught me that protecting an immigrant

---

22 "'Drug Dealers, Criminals, Rapists': What Trump Thinks of Mexicans," *BBC News*, August 31, 2016; Trump, Donald. *Twitter Post*. June 17, 2019.

is protecting life. I'm pro-life because I believe unborn life is the most vulnerable life. Undocumented immigrants are vulnerable too. They have few rights and protections. Barriers prevent them from or scare them away from speaking up for themselves. They are villainized and used as a political chess piece. Through my encounter with immigrants, the topic of immigration was no longer an abstraction to me. I learned that protecting life meant protecting immigrants too.

Teresa's words provided salve to what felt like a wound that I had developed on behalf of my clients; a wound caused by worry and despair. Until I spoke with Teresa, my fear that Luisa and Carmen's babies would trap them had clouded my understanding of the situation. In a similar way, I think that fear often drives our desire to push out immigrants. However, by valuing a person because of their own human dignity, regardless of what they've done or how they got here, we will see how protecting life fosters peace in our communities and in our world.

* * *

As the mother of my son, James, my life is full in a different way than it was before. I'm back at work now, and one of the best parts of my day is walking in the door to our home after work. I exclaim, "JAMES!!!" and he stops what he's doing and waddles up to me with a big open-mouth smile, making me feel like the most important person in the room and in the world.

Being a mom has some challenges. From what I know about Luisa and Carmen's experiences, their trade-off looked different from mine. They had to make sacrifices I didn't have to make, like staying home from school most days to raise their children. They didn't have their parents' support, while both of my parents and my in-laws cleared their schedules to help with James in the first few weeks of his life and continue to offer their support now. Luisa and Carmen didn't have access to the same quality of medical benefits as I did because they weren't legal residents. Their children qualified for food stamps based on their income level. Sometimes, James's grandparents will treat him to a full entree at an upscale restaurant. My clients had to struggle to provide for their children in ways that I haven't had to struggle.

Motherhood is a heavy responsibility for Luisa and Carmen, just as it is for any woman. Poverty, their young age, and their estranged relationships with their parents added pressures to their new role. But I trust that, like me, they have felt the joy of watching their children take their first steps or hearing them say "Mama" for the first time. Being a mom—being James' mom—has ushered a time in my life filled with awesome experiences that I couldn't have had without him.

# CHAPTER SIX

# FEAR

———

When I was working at Grace House, it kept coming up in the news that ICE (U.S. Immigration and Customs Enforcement) would be carrying out raids in the D.C. area. Many of our Latino clients were afraid to leave their homes to go to work or school for fear that they would be deported on the spot.

An immigration lawyer came and spoke to our staff. Seeking ways to help our clients in an atmosphere of fear and chaos, we listened keenly for any direction or explanation from the lawyer. She was a brunette, dressed in business casual attire, and probably in her mid-thirties. Her matter-of-fact way of speaking mirrored her characterization of the raids as "business as usual." It seemed like she was saying, *I know [ICE's] game and I'm going to play them at it.*

"President Obama has deported two million people since the beginning of his presidency, mainly focusing on 'felons not families,'" she said. "Obama is trying to show that his administration can 'do' law enforcement and can seal the border, helping to pave the way for Hilary Clinton's election." *What? Obama deports a lot of people?* I thought. *I don't follow the* news much, and I'm more interested in Republican than Democratic politicians, so this was news to me. *I thought Obama made it easier on immigrants, Why have I never heard this before?* And then I realized, *This is not good news for my clients.*

The lawyer said that, throughout U.S. immigration history, we had "rolled out the red carpet" for immigrants when the economy was great and immigrants were needed for farm and manual labor, and then scapegoated and deported immigrants when the economy took a hit.[23] *That's kind of messed up,* I thought. *But I can see how farms need immigrant workers. I've always heard that most people who work at farms are immigrants.* Even though I was familiar with the idea of immigrants comprising a large percentage of farm jobs (in fact, data shows that 21 percent of farmworkers are Lawful Permanent Residents and 47 percent are undocumented immigrants), to hear the lawyer speak about this as an unofficial, but intentional, immigration policy was new to me.[24]

The lawyer fielded some questions from the staff about what to advise our clients. She explained, "To enter a person's home, ICE must have the name of the individual they are looking for on a signed warrant. Individuals should ask ICE officials to pass any warrant they have under the door in the event that ICE arrives at their home." She continued, "Tell your clients not to open the door if the officer doesn't have a warrant, or if the warrant does not have the individual's name on it. ICE can only interview the person whose name

---

23    Jeff Israely, "As the Global Economy Sinks, Tensions Over Immigration Rise," *Time*, February 6, 2009.

24    "Selected Statistics on Farworkers," *Farmworker Justice,* 2018.

is on the warrant, and they can't deport the person's children without a signed warrant. But they could, in the case of a warrant, deport the individual whose name is on the warrant and they wouldn't necessarily arrange for someone to take care of that person's children in their absence."

When the lawyer finished her presentation, Grace House team managers made a few other announcements and clarified some administrative matters. Then the meeting ended. I didn't discuss what we'd just heard with any of my team members that day; I was a little too stunned.

In a meeting with my team a week or so after the lawyer's presentation, our manager provided us each with handouts that explained to our clients what to do if ICE came to their door, complete with graphics of U.S. ICE officials. The handouts read "Know Your Rights" in big, bold letters across the top of the page. Our manager encouraged us, "I know this is really hard, but given the raids, we have to prepare for the worst. Try to have conversations with your clients about advanced directives—designating who they would want to take care of their kids in the case that they are deported." A verbal directive and, in most cases, a written directive wouldn't necessarily hold legal sway, but it was better than nothing.

I discussed advanced directives with one of my clients. Aware of the question's gravity, I asked in a low voice, "Laura, have you thought of who might take care of your kids if you were deported?"

She looked down, and when she looked back up at me, her eyes were filled with tears. "Yes, I have someone in mind," she said. Then she asked, "Would my written directives have legal weight?"

"I don't know," I said. I gave her a list of legal resources. "If you're interested in speaking with a lawyer, here is a list of legal resources in the area," I said. I had a knot in the pit of my stomach, but I continued, "In the meantime, it would still be a good idea to talk to the person you have in mind, and to write it down."

I understand why some of my clients were afraid to leave their homes. Now that I have a child, it's even harder for me to imagine ICE officials coming to my home or work and sending me to another country before I even have a chance to say goodbye to my son.

Before the immigration lawyer spoke with our team, I didn't see the ways in which immigrants are often scapegoated and manipulated for political gain. Now, I see this trend continuing under President Trump. Trump announced to NBC News in June of 2019, "We have a tremendous problem at the border. We've got people pouring in, and it means crime, it means drugs."[25] This type of rhetoric helped him win the presidency. A *Los Angeles Times* article reported that "surveys show that Trump increased his vote over Mitt Romney's on a number of immigration-related issues" by taking more of a hardline stance on immigration.[26]

---

25   "'It's All Done': President Donald Trump Teases Immigration Deal with Mexico NBC News," *NBC News*, YouTube, June 11, 2019.

26   Philip Klinkner, "Op-Ed: Yes, Trump's Hard-Line Immigration Stance Helped Him Win the Election—But It Could Be His Undoing,"

It makes me mad when politicians use deportation and detention to show that they are tough on crime, or to appeal to their base in other ways.[27] I know that this political stance and rhetoric increases fear among immigrants all over the U.S., many of whom contribute to the economy and follow the law (besides crossing the border illegally). This isn't just politics at stake. Anti-immigrant rhetoric and policy impacts people like Laura, whom I told to write down on a piece of paper who should take her kids if she were deported.

\* \* \*

At the same time that I was scared *for* my clients, I was scared *of* my clients, or at least people "like" them. I had heard that immigrants bring crime and drugs into the country, and I had internalized that information. I hesitated before entering my client's apartment building on a house visit because I thought someone might hurt me or rob me. I was nervous to go inside. It was dirty and the lawn wasn't kept up. The "broken windows theory" that visible signs of crime foster an environment of more crime came to mind.[28] As I mentioned in my Introduction, I, like my mom, wondered if visiting my clients' homes was safe. But it was the middle of the day in a moderately trafficked area not far from the school, so I decided that I would be okay, and I went inside.

---

*Los Angeles Times*, April 17, 2017.

27   Johnny Kauffman, "Georgia Candidate for Governor Doesn't Plan to Use 'Deportation Bus' to Deport Anyone," *NPR*, May 16, 2018.

28   Adam J. McKee, "Broken Windows Theory," *Encylopædia Britannica*, December 14, 2018.

I found my client's apartment unit where he lived with his mom and baby sister and did my introductory spiel: "Hi, my name is Mellie, I work for Grace House and I connect clients with community resources. How can I help you?"

The teenage student looked at me and didn't say anything. His mom spoke first and said, "He won't go to school. He stays in the house all the time. I tell him to go to school, but he won't."

"Okay," I said, and I looked at the student. "Why don't you want to go to school?" Whereas I was afraid to enter the apartment building, I learned that he was afraid to leave the house.

"I don't like it there. And I don't want anything to happen to my family while I'm at school."

My colleagues and I heard this kind of response from many of our clients. Somewhere along the way, I picked up a mantra that I told my clients: "You can't stay home because you're afraid of *them*. That's what *they* want you to do. *They* want you to stay home from work, or school, or wherever it is that you need to go, so that fear alone will cripple you and keep you from functioning."

Who are *They*? *They* are people who want to scare you. For my clients, *They* were ICE.

"We'll be okay," his mom said. "But you have to go to school." His mom wanted him to get out of the house; she felt that he was wasting his life.

I explained to the student, "It's good for you to go to school. That's why your mom wants you to go." He nodded. As I was leaving, I thought, *Maybe he'll start going to school, and I'll see him around.* But I never did see him at Central.

After doing the house visits and equipping myself with the data about immigration and crime, I see now that my fear was largely based on misinformation. I didn't know at the time that immigrants have a lower criminal incarceration rate than the average American, and not the other way around.[29] I would love to say that, equipped with this knowledge, I have wiped my mind clean of any racial or class bias or prejudice. But that isn't true. What I can say is that by making myself aware of those prejudices, I am striving to overcome them.

---

29   Alex Nowraseth, "Illegal Immigrants and Crime—Assessing the Evidence," *Cato Institute*, March 4, 2019.

## CHAPTER SEVEN

# KINSHIP

———

Merriam Webster defines kin as a "group of persons of common ancestry."[30] It lists synonyms for kinship as an affinity, association, or connection.[31] Camila was one of the few clients whom I met with outside of work. We visited each other's homes, met each other's families, and exchanged personal phone numbers. I felt a special kinship with her.

On my last day of work at Grace House, Paul and I waited for Camila on the curb in front of my house. I had found the house two years prior on Craigslist, and I lived there with three roommates. My client, Camila, hadn't been to my house before, and I didn't want her to miss it. I was moving back to Atlanta the next day and had arranged to give her my bedding, lamps, bike, some clothes, and other household items. It was hot and swampy, as D.C. tends to be in the summer, and the houses around us conveyed signs of a

---

30   *Merriam-Webster.com Dictionary*, s.v. "kin," accessed January 31, 2020.

31   *Merriam-Webster.com Dictionary*, s.v. "kinship," accessed January 31, 2020.

gentrifying neighborhood: the house across the street had a boarded-up window while the neighbors a few houses down had a manicured green lawn.

We waited for Camila for forty-five minutes after our agreed-upon time. *Where is she??* I wondered. *I hope she's okay, that she's not lost or that something happened to her.* And then, the selfish part of my brain, the one that I have to stuff down lest it come out and embarrass me, asked, *How am I going to get rid of my things if she doesn't show up?* At last Camila, her sister, three-year-old daughter, and the man driving them arrived in an old red van with fading letters spelling the name of a Spanish church. We made quick, jovial introductions. Paul, not having used his Spanish in a while, answered Camila's questions with a smile saying, "Si, si, si."

\* \* \*

My colleague referred Camila to me in the spring, so I only met with her on a few occasions before leaving D.C. She was sweet and had a bubbly personality. She emigrated from El Salvador and had a young child in the U.S. She told me she was expecting two more teenage children, a daughter and a son, to come from El Salvador soon. She left El Salvador, a country mired with high unemployment rates, gang violence, and corruption, in search of a better life for herself and her children in the U.S.[32] Her wide-eyed expression and quiet, but excited, voice conveyed both her eagerness to reunite

---

32   Menjívar, Cecilia and Andrea Gomez Cervantes, "El Salvador: Civil War, Natural Disasters, and Gang Violence Drive Migration," *Migration Policy Institute,* August 29, 2018.

with them and anxiety about their journey. At our first meeting, she asked me to help her find out whether her teenage children could attend summer camp at their future high school once they arrived. I made a few calls and did some research for her. She didn't know exactly when they would be coming, so I suspected that she had sent money for them to get help crossing the border and that she was waiting to hear of their whereabouts.

Despite the high costs and risks of crossing the border illegally, the journey is not unique to Camila's children. A Homeland Security Operational Analysis Center study reports that "the flow of unlawful migrants from the NT [Northern Triangle countries of El Salvador, Honduras, and Guatemala] to the United States in 2017 could have ranged from about 218,000 to about 345,000 between POEs [ports of entry]."[33] Migrants often hire a coyote, or human smuggler, "to lead the way across the frontier for a price, with higher prices generally increasing the odds of a successful entry."[34] While crossing the border illegally is dangerous and may lead to deportation or detention, many of my clients made the journey. The opportunity for a better life in the U.S. outweighed the risks.

---

33    Greenfield, Victoria, Blas Nuñez-Neto, Ian Mitch, Joseph C. Chang, and Etienne Rosas, "Human Smuggling and Associated Revenues: What Do or Can We Know About Routes from Central America to the United States?" *Homeland Security Operational Analysis Center, Rand Corporation,* 2019.

34    Massey, Douglas S., Jorge Durand, and Karen A. Pren, "Why Border Enforcement Backfired," *The University of Chicago Press,* 2016: 1564.

\* \* \*

Once Camila arrived with the driver and her family, we started transferring things from the house to the car. When she told me that she had hired the driver to transport my things, I thought, *Wow. I thought my clients didn't have—or wouldn't spend—money on hired services like this one.* It was foolish of me to think that I knew how my clients would or wouldn't use their resources. It showed me that there was still a lot I didn't know about my clients.

After we transferred everything, Camila and her crew loaded into the car. Paul and I planned to meet them at her apartment so I could give her my bike. When we arrived there, I saw that she had set up mattresses on the floor for her children that she was waiting on. I imagine that she must have been so anxious, wondering where they were and how they were doing. But her desire to be with them and the prevalence of poverty and violence in her home country outweighed the risks of her children's journey. We wished her luck, she thanked us, and I came back home to a bare room and moved back to Atlanta the next day.

I recently reached out to Camila to see how she and her family were doing. "It's so good to hear from you," she said. "Gracias a Dios" (Thanks be to God)—she was reunited with her children. She texted me a picture of her teenage daughter, who shares Camila's brown hair and plum lip color, on her high school graduation day. Her daughter is smiling in the photo, wearing her graduation hat and white robe. "I'm so happy to see you all happy," she said when I sent her a picture of me with Paul and our son, James. "God bless you all," she said.

I'm happy that I was able to give Camila some of my belongings, and as is often the case with service, Camila returned the gift back to me in the form of kinship and the sense of self-identity that comes along with it.

\* \* \*

During my time at Grace House, I formed special bonds with Latino immigrants in my community. Camila was one of them. Sonia was another.

When speaking with Sonia, with her easy smile and her calming brown eyes, it would be hard to perceive the darkness that had descended on her home in the few months before I met her. Sonia reached out for help to one of the social workers at Washington Elementary, who referred her to me. Sonia was in her forties and her granddaughter went to Washington, one of the schools that I worked at due to its partnership with Grace House. Albeit a young grandmother, Sonia wore the years of experience in her graying hair and wise resolve, the way that grandmothers often do. Her brother, Marcelo, had worked for a moving company in Virginia. He fell off a moving truck while on the job and his coworkers abandoned him at a Virginia emergency room. When the medical staff got to him, he was unconscious. He was then moved to a hospice where the hospice staff's failure to rotate him left him with inflamed, oozing bed sores.

Eventually, after a considerable amount of time, the hospice staff tracked down Marcelo's family. Even though Sonia hadn't seen her brother in over a decade, she retrieved him— still in a coma—from the hospice and brought him to her home. Marcelo's wife and young daughter were still in El Salvador, so Sonia helped arrange for them to come to D.C. She hoped that Marcelo's wife would help take care of him once they were reunited.

Marcelo's wife and daughter arrived in D.C., but they had been apart for so many years that they had grown estranged from one another. Family separation and the trauma that goes along with it was common among my clients at Grace House. Even before the Trump administration, family separation has been a trend throughout the history of U.S. immigration policy.[35] In Marcelo's case, time and circumstance dissolved his marriage. As months passed, Sonia realized that she would be Marcelo's only caretaker.

Marcelo was undocumented and was not insured, which is common among noncitizens. The Henry J. Kaiser Family Foundation states, "Noncitizens are significantly more likely than citizens to be uninsured. Among the nonelderly population, 23% of lawfully present immigrants and more than four in ten (45%) undocumented immigrants are uninsured compared to less than one in ten (8%) citizens." Immigrants are less-often insured due to the lack of employer-provided benefits, inability to afford private insurance, and inability to access government-funded health insurance.[36] The lack

---

35   Natalie Escobar, "Family Separation Isn't New: U.S. Immigration Policy Has Traumatized Migrant Children and Parents for Nearly a Century," *The Atlantic*, August 14, 2018.

36   "Health Coverage of Immigrants," *The Henry J. Kaiser Family Foundation*, February 15, 2019.

of insurance limits undocumented citizens from receiving the same quality of care that an insured individual receives.

I went on a house visit to Sonia's home, and I saw Marcelo lying on a cot in the back room of their house, comatose and gaunt. I was horrified to see him in this state. I couldn't believe my eyes; I thought, *There's no way that this is the best care that we can provide in the U.S.* Sonia told me that it had been months since a physician had examined Marcelo, and she was concerned about his condition. She wanted to get help for her brother. She had legal status, but she was afraid to go to the hospital because some of her family, Marcelo included, were not citizens. Like Sonia, even individuals who qualify for benefits often fear getting the help they need because of their citizenship status or a loved one's status. They are afraid that if they bring attention to themselves or ask for some type of public benefit—they will get deported.[37]

I surveyed the situation. I could tell that Sonia was scared and was looking to me to make a decision. Me, a twenty-four-year-old woman, with one and a half years of work experience out of college, with no background in health care. I was scared. I was scared that if we called 911 that Sonia's brother or other family members could be deported, and that if we didn't call, Marcelo would starve to death in her home. Sonia's fear for her brother's life mounted over the fear of threats to her status, so we called 911. That experience of her asking for my guidance, and us making the joint decision, bonded us. We acted together on Marcelo's behalf.

_____
37   Ibid.

An ambulance came and took Sonia and Marcelo to the hospital. The hospital staff *were* able to do something for him there, even if it was just the doctor showing compassion for Sonia and Marcelo.

I asked Sonia, "How did the visit go?"

"Very well," she said, with a peaceful smile. "The doctor was very nice to us."

My parents have told me and my siblings many times, "You all are family. You have to take care of each other." Perhaps we need this reminder because sometimes it's easier to *not* take care of each other. But when we do, it creates a ripple effect. Sonia took care of her brother, and the doctor took care of Sonia. Through their compassion for one another, they formed the bonds of kinship.

It seemed like the visit encouraged Sonia. She seemed more hopeful than before, and more assured that she was giving her brother the best care. There were a few signs of progress and moments of joy after their hospital visit. One day, Sonia was sitting at Marcelo's bedside eating an orange slice. He turned toward her, moved his head side to side and grunted, "Mmm," seeming to gesture that he wanted some of the orange. At one point, he even laughed.

Because of Marcelo's health struggles, the role of caretaker was taking a toll on Sonia. She was a selfless, dedicated caretaker and spent hours by his bedside, rotating him, giving him fluids, and cleaning him. She needed a support system and a way to digest the trauma that she had experienced. I was able to provide some support for a few months through therapy lite sessions (therapeutic strategies that I had learned during my time at Grace House), but oftentimes immigrants and their children don't receive the mental health services they need. One study of Asian and Latino immigrants found that only 6 percent of immigrants had ever received mental health care, making them 40 percent less likely than U.S.-born participants to access services.[38] It is critical that these individuals receive the care that they need to be fully functioning in their lives and in their communities.

Sonia and I met in my office one day. That day, I just wanted to focus on Sonia and what *she* needed. I had only been working with Grace House for about six months at this point and had no background in mental health, so many of the activities I taught my clients I either knew from my personal life or had learned in training during one of the school-based mental health team's professional development meetings. There was one activity that I really liked: I led her in a mindfulness exercise that involved illustrating on paper what she wanted to see happen in her life. In her picture, Sonia drew two birds flying together, and she explained that the birds were her and her brother.

I pictured Sonia sitting by Marcelo's bed at all hours of the day and night, making sure he was breathing and getting

---

38    Lee, SungKyu and Jason Matejkowski, "Mental Health Service Utilization Among Noncitizens in the United States: Findings from the National Latino and Asian American Study," *Administration and Policy in Mental Health and Mental Health Services Research*, September 2012: 406-418.

enough fluids, and waiting for any sign of acknowledgment from him. I asked her if, in a way, they were already like two birds flying together, side by side. She started crying, smiled, and said, "Yes."

# CHAPTER EIGHT

# ACCEPTANCE

———

Outside of work, there were two spheres of my community where I spent a lot of time—my church, St. Monica's; and Nelson Recreation Center. Diverse groups of people gathered at these places for distinct reasons. At both of these places, I found people who welcomed me in, even though I looked different and had a different background from them.

\* \* \*

Paul and I shared a favorite activity when we lived in D.C.: walking. That Saturday was like any other in terms of us going for a stroll through Paul's neighborhood, a culturally and racially diverse area in northwest D.C. What was different about that day was that we started hearing voices—singing—and seeing large groups of people walking toward us. They were men, women, and children, mostly Latino, carrying colorful, ornate floats of the Virgin Mary. They sang in Spanish, hailing "Maria, Maria, Maria." I remembered it had been announced at our church, St. Monica's, that the feast day of Our Lady of Guadalupe was coming up. We had just found our way into the procession from St. Monica's to the National Shrine a few miles down the road.

We walked with the procession a few blocks. "Do you want to keep going?" Paul asked. We decided to continue and for the next hour or so we joined parishioners, nuns, and priests, singing all the way until we finally arrived at the Shrine. I had seen a similar parade before, in Sevilla, Spain during the Semana Santa (Holy Week) festivities. I traveled there specifically to witness the famous processions. But here I was in my own town, joining a procession myself. I didn't have to go anywhere exotic to experience the richness of a culture different from my own; it was right down the street.

Diversity is a common buzzword in the workplace and universities. Moving beyond those spheres, data shows that diversity strengthens communities. One study showed that "people who lived in more racially diverse zip codes were more likely to offer help to those in need after the [2013 Boston Marathon] bombings."[39] Living in a diverse community and attending a church with a diverse congregation helped me grow. It showed me new manifestations of the many faces of God as well as the similarities I shared with people of different backgrounds and ethnicities. Through our church, I saw how first- and second-generation Latino immigrants made the church community and my personal faith journey stronger.

Being surrounded by a diverse group of people at St. Monica's Easter Vigil mass allowed me to experience my faith

---

39   Jayanth Narayanan, "Diversity Is Good for Our Communities. Here's the Evidence," *World Economic Forum*, 2018.

in a palpable way. Paul was with his family in Michigan for Easter, so I decided to attend the Easter Vigil at church by myself. The church was jam-packed and Mass was said in four different languages: English, Spanish, Haitian Creole, and Vietnamese. The service started off with the lights dim, but as we celebrated Jesus' resurrection, the lights came on and illuminated the church. The priest baptized over fifty adults and children, and the band played a song in Spanish about being "washed by the water of Jesus." A few rows in front of me and to the left, a thin brunette lady sang and danced to the song. She mimed with her hands that water was flowing over her. I watched the lady dance with joy and it brought me joy. She stood alone in her dance, but I felt united with her and the congregation in her celebration of Easter.

Also at St. Monica's, Paul convinced me to teach a Sunday school class with him. From August through May, we were in charge of teaching the catechism to ten elementary school students, many of whom were second-generation immigrants. Paul and I both attended Catholic school from kindergarten through college, and it was difficult to cram all that we had learned into an hour-long class that met once a week. The students had a lot of questions. One student, Gladys, was Latina and lived with her cousins because her mother had died.

"Why does God let people die?" she asked.

Paul and I tossed the question around and provided some kind of answer. But—*why does God let people die?* I still ask myself at times. Believers of any ethnic background or language may ask this question. Through teaching the class, I noticed similarities like this one between myself and the students, even though we had different backgrounds and traditions.

My understanding of "church in community" expanded through partaking in diverse holiday traditions at St. Monica's. At Christmastime, our church organized Posadas, nightly processions that relive Mary and Joseph's search for shelter. Posada, meaning "inn" or "lodging," is a Mexican tradition that Hispanics and non-Hispanics have adopted in the U.S. When I asked the church organizer if I could invite friends, she said, "The more the merrier! The Posadas are actually open to the public. Anyone who comes, we need to provide hospitality!" I loved how open our church was, starting with the leadership and trickling down to the parishioners. The Posada that Paul and I attended involved Christmas carols and a potluck dinner. A woman who had emigrated from the Philippines brought a traditional Filipino noodle dish and we drank horchata and cider.

The same Filipina woman attended a prayer class with us on a separate occasion. She shared, "My husband and children are in the process of immigrating to the US. I haven't seen my children in four years. I'm preparing for their arrival. I am so excited to see them, but I am nervous too. I don't know what it will be like to have them here. I'm praying for God's grace during this time."

I heard in her story her mixed emotions—the excitement to reunite with her family as well as the fear of the unknown. I hadn't considered her position before. I understood how much I would miss my family if I were in her shoes, and how strange it would be to try to return to "normal" after four years of being apart from them. I appreciated her vulnerability when sharing her feelings with us, and how she was trying to be faithful through the process.

All of these little moments added to my love for our church and our church community. The diverse backgrounds of the parishioners helped me grow in my faith and showed me different manifestations of God. Whether it was the singing and walking of the procession, the dancing at the Easter vigil, or the fellowship at the Posada—all of these venues gave me a new way to engage with others and with God. And yet, in the midst of all of this diversity, I still found similarities: the yearning to make sense of death and darkness like the question that Gladys asked, and the desire to be with family like the Filipina woman who awaited her family's arrival. In all of these ways, my immigrant neighbors made the church community stronger and allowed for me to go deeper in my faith.

\* \* \*

In Gregory Boyle's book, *Tattoos on the Heart,* he writes, "We all need to see that we are in each other's 'jurisdictions,' spheres of acceptance—only, all the time."[40] In my church community, I felt accepted by, and accepting of, the diverse group of parishioners. Despite our diverse ethnicities and ages, we were united by our common faith.

During this time of letting others into my jurisdiction and them letting me into theirs, another part of my community shaped my life experience: my involvement at Nelson

---

40   Gregory Boyle, *Tattoos on the Heart,* New York: Free Press, 2010: 130.

Recreation Center. As I guess many rec center and gym stories go, it was a fitness goal that led me there.

When I was still working for GameDay, I decided I wanted to get in shape so I went to a corporate gym located near me. "I'm interested in a gym membership," I told the person at the front desk. A few moments later, I was meeting with a trainer, an African American man in his forties who was in peak physical form. After asking me about my fitness goals and running through some exercises with me, he said, "I can get you on a training plan that will help you see results. With access to all of the facilities, it will be $130 per month. Your first month is free." *Well, that was not what I was expecting,* I thought as I left the gym and walked home. *And it's so expensive!*

I discussed it with another GameDay coach, Simone, when she came to help me out at Washington the next day. When I told her the price, her eyes went wide. "What? Girl, that is expensive. My gym is much cheaper than that." But Simone lived in Maryland. *Where am I going to find a cheap gym near me?* I thought.

Around this time, we started the basketball season at GameDay, which meant recruiting a team of fourth and fifth grade girls to play teams from other schools where my GameDay colleagues were coaches. A few of the basketball games were at Nelson Recreation Center, around the corner from where I lived. On my way from the lobby to the basketball court, I noticed a small workout room with treadmills and weight-lifting machines. I approached the man at the front desk, whose nametag said "Mr. G."

"Excuse me," I said. "I'm here for work right now, but I was wondering if the workout room is open to the public?"

"Oh yeah," he said. "As long as you have some type of proof that you live in D.C., you can use any of the rec facilities. The workout room is $15 a month." *Yes!* I thought. *I am cancelling that expensive gym membership.* And I did.

I started going to the workout room at Nelson a few days a week after work. Mr. G often manned the desk. One Wednesday I showed up, and while I was signing in, I heard hip hop music blaring from the speakers upstairs. "What's going on up there?" I asked Mr. G.

"Oh, they have Zumba up there. You can go, if you want. All the classes here are free." I walked up the stairs and peered through the glass plate in the door. There were more than forty women inside grapevining (a dance move that involves a side step sequence similar to footwork used in the foxtrot, polka, or the Electric Slide) and clapping to the right, then to the left.

Almost all of them were African American and looked to be in their thirties and forties. Some were in their fifties. They were having a blast following the instructor, a woman who danced bigger than any of them and yelled out, "Come on, ladies!" from the front.

I walked back downstairs to the workout room and ran on the treadmill. Before I left, I asked Mr. G., "What time does Zumba start?"

"Wednesday nights at six," he said.

The next Wednesday, and most Wednesdays between then and a year and a half later when I moved home to Atlanta, I was at Zumba at 6:00 p.m. Diamond, the instructor, would blast songs like "Fireball" and have us march in place. "Oh, those little steps are cute," she would say. "You gotta take big steps, come on ladies!" she would shout.

I learned that Diamond taught spinning on Friday nights and Piloxing (Pilates plus boxing) on Saturday mornings. Her sidekick, Nikki, attended almost every class. Like at work, I was one of the only white people at Diamond's fitness classes. But having Diamond and Nikki there, I felt comfortable. I gravitated to wherever Nikki was, which meant I danced up in the front row at Zumba, and boxed in the front line at Piloxing. I loved Diamond's classes. It got to the point that Piloxing on Saturday mornings was one of my favorite things about the weekend.

I would leave the rec center in the group of other women, all of us sweating at least a little bit. If Mr. G was still at the desk, I would tell him "Thank you, have a good night!" before walking out the door.

One night when I came into Nelson, Mr. G was at the desk. I overheard him talking about the shirts he made. "You make shirts?" I asked. "That's neat. What kind?"

Mr. G replied, "Oh, I like to make them personalized for people. As a matter of fact, I'll make you one. Can you spell out your name for me?"

"Okay, that's really nice of you, are you sure?" I replied.

"Oh yeah," he said, "I like to do it." I spelled my name out—M-E-L-L-I-E—on a piece of paper.

"I'll get that made for you," he said. *I don't need a shirt, but it's really nice that he wants to make me one. I wonder if he'll actually do it,* I thought.

Pretty soon after that, I stopped seeing Mr. G. at Nelson. I asked the woman who replaced him, Chloe, "What happened to Mr. G?"

"Oh, he's working at another rec center now. There was some re-organization." *Darn, I thought. I'll miss seeing him around.* I continued going to Diamond's classes, and Chloe became the new familiar face.

The weather got warmer, and I switched out my sweatpants for athletic shorts at work. One day on the way home from Washington Elementary, I noticed my reflection in the plastic shelter of a bus stop. *Woah, my legs look really toned. I guess Diamond's classes are paying off.* I walked into Nelson later that afternoon. Chloe was at the desk. "Girl, you look great!" she said, and I blushed. "Thank you!" I said smiling, and signed in.

Months later, I decided to try out a new rec center because they offered a yoga class there. I opened the steel door and walked into the empty lobby. Mr. G walked out of an office. "Mr. G!" I said.

Immediately, he recognized me. "Hey there," he said.

"We've missed you around Nelson. I'm here for the yoga class," I explained.

"You know, hold on a minute, I have something for you," he said. *No way,* I thought. *He really made me a shirt? And he's been holding on to it to give it to me? That is so sweet!* He retreated into his office. A few moments later he returned with a white T-shirt in his hand. "I've had this for months," he said, handing it to me. It had my name written in glitter glue across the front, outlined by blue and gold stars. I walked home that night, personalized T-shirt in hand, with the giddy feeling of being accepted.

* * *

While I benefited from being accepted in my community, it was devastating to see how a denial of that acceptance impacted my clients. I worked with clients who were not accepted at the national level or in their school community based on their legal status or ethnicity. A colleague shared with me, "We see some of our clients join gangs because the gang members are the only ones who ask them how they're doing."

While working at Grace House and living in the same neighborhood as many of my clients, I learned that acceptance is crucial to moving forward in the sphere of immigration. By accepting each other, we will be better able to identify and work toward common goals. Acceptance will build a firm foundation for our communities and our nation.

# CHAPTER NINE

# LOVE

---

My brother, Victor, is three years younger than me. Once, when I was a high school junior and he was an eighth grader, he was bothering our older sister Caroline in some way—I don't remember exactly how. "If you don't stop," I threatened, "I'm not going to drive you home from school tomorrow." He didn't listen.

The next day, I got a text from Victor as I drove away from the school. "Where are you," it said.

"Find a ride," I responded, and drove away.

This was not one of our finest moments as brother and sister. But then there were all the mornings (every morning) when I woke Victor up for school and turned on the shower for him. And there was the text he sent me when I was studying abroad in Spain: "You are such a role model to me ... you are so good at everything you do. I don't know how you do it, sometimes it even makes me mad." He may ignore me and I may leave him at school, but at the end of the day, we love each other and take care of each other. We do certain things for the people we love.

I loved my client, Mario. He crossed the southwest border without friends or family. I met him when he was a Central High School student from El Salvador. He was sixteen, had brown hair, and was a little on the shorter side. Mario worked as a line cook at a restaurant after school and on the weekends. A few burn scars lined his arms and hands. He had a melancholic demeanor and during quiet moments in my office, when recalling the time he spent in a Texas detention center or lamenting his school troubles, he would look down at his long fingernails and pick at them. He reminded me of Victor, and he felt like an adopted brother or cousin to me. When he came to my office to ask me for help, it felt like it was Victor asking me for help. I would get that warm and cozy feeling that I got when Victor called me to ask for advice. But that feeling would wane when the conversation ended, and I realized that my brother, real or adopted, would have to make the decision on his own.

It was awkward for me to ask a client whether they had legal status. It felt like I was asking them, "Do you have a right to be here?" when all *I* had done to be here was be born. So, I avoided that question unless it was pertinent to my work. With every client, I went through the list of resources that I could provide them. When meeting with Mario, I gave him the usual spiel: "I can help you access resources for food, shelter, health, work, legal services ..."

"I need legal resources, Miss," he said. "I have a court date coming up, and I want to be able to stay here." Like many of my clients, Mario had been released from the Texas detention center after a few weeks, but he was given an order to appear in court on a specific date. Typically, these court dates were months—sometimes even years—later. That court decision would determine whether he could stay in the U.S. or be deported.

There were no pro bono resources available for Mario, so I helped him meet with a fee-for-service immigration lawyer. After they met for the first time, Mario told me, "It's very expensive, Miss, but I liked him and he was nice." The lawyer informed him that his best chance of receiving legal status was to file for Special Immigrant Juvenile Status (SIJS). SIJS is granted to individuals who can prove that they have been abused, neglected, or abandoned by a parent.

"Is that true?" I asked. "Were you neglected?"

"Kind of," he said. I didn't press him on the issue. I knew that there weren't many options for him to apply for legal status. For individuals who do not have immediate relatives residing legally in the U.S. and who are not highly skilled, the wait time to receive status "approaches infinity," except for in special cases like SIJS.[41]

Mario's court date was approaching and his lawyer was scheduled to go with him. But the night before his court summons, D.C. was hit with several feet of snow and everything closed down. I was holed up inside at a friend's apartment, preparing to have a staycation until the storm passed, but I had brought my work phone just in case Mario called

---

41    Flynn, Mike, Shikha Dalmia, and Terry Colon, "What Part of Legal Immigration Don't You Understand?" *Reason Magazine*, October 2008.

me. His lawyer wasn't sure whether the court would be open and Mario wasn't able to get through the court's phone system to find out, so he went to the court to be sure. He called me afterward. "It's closed, Miss" he said. "My lawyer said that my court date would be rescheduled." I was relieved that he had gone to the court just in case, but I felt sorry for him trekking through the snow on his own. I didn't know much about how the court system worked, but I knew that missing your court summons could be cause for deportation.

After the snowstorm passed, Mario's court date was rescheduled for months later. During the waiting period, Mario was often discouraged. School was hard for him and legal fees cost him a large percentage of his restaurant paycheck. Some days Mario would say, "I'm tired of this," or "I don't know what I'm doing," or "I don't know if this is going to work." All the while, he continued going to school and working at the restaurant. Some days, he was too tired from the night shift to come to school.

I couldn't imagine what Mario was going through. I never worked during the school year when I was in high school, and I always came home to a warm house and my family. Here, Mario was sixteen years old, working to pay for his rent, food, and lawyer—all while sending money to his family in El Salvador. He worked at a restaurant in Chinatown, maybe even one that I ate at with my friends. There was something nonsensical about him contributing to the labor force but only having a chance to gain legal status through proving that his parents had abused or neglected him.

* * *

Mario's experience demonstrates the experience many immigrants go through to stay and work legally in the U.S. Due to the danger of gangs and unrest in his hometown, he traveled from El Salvador by himself. Many individuals from the Northern Triangle countries of El Salvador, Guatemala, and Honduras have made a journey similar to Mario's. Cato Institute reports, "Northern Triangle citizens account for 75 percent of all Border Patrol apprehensions" in FY 2019.[42] The same report says, "A major difference between the apprehension of Mexicans in the past and those from the Northern Triangle today is that the latter are turning themselves into Border Patrol to ask for asylum while the former were trying to evade."[43] I imagine that Mario was happy to encounter Border Patrol. It meant that his walk through the desert was over.

When I left D.C., Mario was awaiting his court date and the next steps with his lawyer. Later on, I was happy to learn from a former colleague that Mario graduated from high school.

I loved Mario like a brother. I didn't want him to be deported, but I couldn't "protect" him, in some of the same ways as well as in different (systemic) ways, that I can't protect my brother Victor. Mario made strides on his own to get protection, yet

42  Alex Nowraseth, "1.3 Percent of All Central Americans in the Northern Triangle Were Apprehended by Border Patrol This Fiscal Year—So Far," *Cato Institute*, June 7, 2019.

43  Ibid.

he still faced barriers to achieving legal status. On a national scale, I can't help but wonder what it would be like if we saw immigrants as our brothers and sisters. Maybe we would kick them out of the car. But we wouldn't kick them out of the country. We would love them too much to do that.

# CONCLUSION

After months of considering law schools in Michigan (where Paul's family lives) or Atlanta (where my family lives), Paul and I decided to move to Atlanta so that he could start law school at Georgia State. I was excited about the move because it meant living in the same city as my family. However, leaving Grace House was bittersweet; I cared so much about my clients, but because of the systemic barriers that they faced and my own inexperience, I often felt hopeless in my job.

As for my law school trajectory, I got into several law schools but decided not to go because my heart wasn't in it. While I wanted to work in some type of service role, I didn't want to work with immigrants anymore due to how emotionally drained I was from my time as a community support worker. I felt disillusioned by the American dream because it seemed so hard for my clients to attain. I felt unable to help my clients climb out of the hole that they were in and felt guilty that my whiteness, my privilege, my American-ness kept me out of that hole.

My parents were initially confused and disappointed that I decided against law school because they thought that I had been really excited about it. In hindsight, I wish that I had shared with them earlier on that I was unsure about going, but I didn't want to let them down. As time went on and we talked about it more, they moved on too. They were thrilled that we would be moving back to Atlanta for Paul to start law school.

A few weeks after moving home, I asked my mom if we could take a trip to Europe that summer. She smiled and said, "For some reason, I had a feeling you might ask me that." Within a few days, we booked our flight to Italy. The irony was not lost on me that we had just booked a trip on somewhat of a whim that would have been out of the question for my clients due to financial and legal constraints. After the trip, I redirected myself career-wise and started working in a new field.

***

Fast-forward to a few years later when I decided to write this book. When I told a good friend that I was writing about immigrants and immigration, she said, "Don't tell my mom. She thinks you're a Democrat."

*Your mom is so judgmental!* I thought. *Oh no, not a Democrat!* I went on in my head, with heavy sarcasm. *It's okay for* me *to call out Democrats because* I'm *a conservative but I have liberal views on some things, but not your mom, because she is* really *Republican and she* loves *Donald Trump.* I drew a line in my head of what level of conservatism was okay, and my friend's mom had crossed that line. Then I realized: *Who's being more judgmental here? Me or my friend's mom?* Me judging someone else's politics for judging my politics doesn't help anyone, and it doesn't lead to any solutions.

There have been other instances when political allegiances have clouded my own judgment. On a hot summer day, a few weeks after the first 2020 presidential debates, I was walking down the street in a residential neighborhood of Atlanta. I passed a sign on a neighbor's recycling bin that spelled out in thick permanent marker, "Only Nazis and pedophiles put kids in cages." It annoyed me and made me mad, and I thought, *You probably don't realize that kids were put in cages during the Obama administration!*[44]

I slowed my pace and started frantically googling, "Kids in cages during the Obama administration." Within seconds, I found a tweet from Donald Trump. "Democrats had to quickly take down a tweet called "Kids in Cages, Inhumane Treatment at the Border," because the horrible picture used was from the Obama years. Very embarrassing!"[45]

*See, liberal neighbor!* I thought, feeling justified. *Who's a pedophile or Nazi now??* However, my satisfaction was short-lived. My higher self crept in. *Okay, Mellie, what's your point? That if Obama and Trump both put kids in cages, now it's*

---

44   Miriam Valverde, "Fact-checking Biden on Use of Cages for Immigrants During Obama Administration," *Politifact*, September 13, 2019.

45   Tal Axelrod, "Trump Knocks Dems for Tweeting Obama-Era 'Kids in Cages' Photo," *The Hill*, July 11, 2019.

*okay? That doesn't change the fact that kids are still in cages.*
My lower self said: *Be quiet, higher self.*

I agree with the poster writer's sentiment that kids shouldn't be put in cages. However, instead of nodding my head in agreement when I read the sign, I interpreted it as an attack on my political party and therefore an attack on me, and I turned around and pointed the finger at the Obama administration. My response was based on politics, and it didn't take immigrants' lives into account. Part of me is glad that Trump pointed out that kids were in cages during the Obama Administration. The other, more compassionate, part of me realizes that this game of tossing up responsibility like a hot potato slows any progress toward an immigration policy that recognizes immigrants as humans.

DHS Secretary Jeh Johnson's interview with Real Clear Politics further demonstrates how partisanship hinders our ability to find solutions around the topic of immigration. Johnson was appointed as DHS secretary during the Obama administration. The interviewer said, "I'm not playing the political blame game, I'm talking about issues and one of them, the president says … is a measure that was written by Democratic Senator Dianne Feinstein in 2008 that became law."[46] The interviewer went straight from saying he wouldn't play the blame game to blaming Feinstein in the same sentence. In this divisive environment, it's difficult to find solutions or compromise on immigration policy because everyone is either attacking or being attacked.

---

46   Tim Hains, "Obama DHS Sec. Jeh Johnson: I Freely Admit We Detained Children, 'It Was Necessary," *Real Clear Politics*, June 24, 2018.

Pointing out that immigration is a political issue is not a breakthrough. But, reactions like my own to a neighbor's hand-written poster clarify why it's so hard for any compromise or change to happen regarding immigration. It's not Trump's fault, or Obama's fault, or the media's fault that kids are in cages. But it is my fault when I focus more on the politics of the issue than the issue itself. That kind of defense mechanism or political loyalty only perpetuates the problem. By going beyond the politics and focusing on the matter at hand—in this case, the matter at hand being young children's lives—I might actually be part of the solution.

I know I don't have all the answers and that I still fall into the partisan mindset at times, but I'm trying to advocate for immigration as a humanist despite that. My hope is that this book will shed light on the immigration debate by illustrating an image of immigrants that is different from the violent, negative image often depicted in the news. I believe that putting a new face on the topic of immigration will lead to a shift in the way that we think about the issue—from a focus on politics to a focus on people.

I'm not alone in my advocacy for immigrants. Seventy-six percent of people say immigration is good for the country.[47] At some point, I hope that that belief aligns with the way that we welcome immigrants into our own communities.

My work with immigrants changed my political perspective on immigration to a more compassionate view on the

47  "In Depth: Topics A to Z: Immigration," *Gallup*, 2020.

issue, even though I still associate myself as a political conservative. I don't expect people to read my book and wake up the next day with a compassionate view on immigration. But I do hope that my book will lead readers to ask themselves, "Why *do* I feel the way I do about immigrants?" And that is an important question.

# APPENDIX

---

## Introduction

"Asylum Decisions and Denials Jump in 2018." *TRAC Immigration.* November 29, 2018, https://trac.syr.edu/immigration/reports/539/.

Frazee, Gretchen. "4 Myths About How Immigrants Affect the U.S. Economy." *PBS News Hour.* November 2, 2018, .

Gonzalez, Daniel. "The 2019 Migrant Surge is Unlike Any We've Seen Before. This Is Why." *USA Today.* September 25, 2019, https://www.usatoday.com/in-depth/news/nation/2019/09/23/immigration-issues-migrants-mexico-central-america-caravans-smuggling/2026215001/.

Gonzalez, David. "In Today's Headlines, Echoes of Central America's Proxy Wars of the 1980s." *The New York Times.* February 27, 2019, https://www.nytimes.com/2019/02/27/lens/finding-echoes-of-todays-headlines-in-central-americas-proxy-wars-in-the-1980s.html.

"In Depth: Topics A to Z: Immigration." *Gallup.* 2020, https://news.gallup.com/poll/1660/immigration.aspx.

Kauffman, Johnny. "Georgia Candidate for Governor Doesn't Plan to Use 'Deportation Bus' to Deport Anyone." NPR. May 16, 2018, https://www.npr.org/2018/05/16/611680288/georgia-candidate-for-governor-doesnt-plan-to-use-deportation-bus-to-deport-anyo.

Mark, Michelle. "More People Are Moving From the US to Mexico than the Other Way Around." *Business Insider.* May 30, 2019, https://www.businessinsider.com/number-of-people-moving-from-us-to-mexico-2019-5.

Nowraseth, Alex. "Illegal Immigrants and Crime—Assessing the Evidence." *Cato Institute.* March 4, 2019, https://www.cato.org/blog/illegal-immigrants-crime-assessing-evidence.

Nunn, Ryan, Jimmy O'Donnell, and Jay Shambaugh. "A Dozen Facts About Immigration." *Brookings.* October 9, 2018, https://www.brookings.edu/research/a-dozen-facts-about-immigration/.

Schmitt, Angie. "The Campaign to Fix Atlanta's Most Dangerous Street and Preserve Its Immigrant Cultures." *StreetsBlog USA.* September 21, 2017, https://usa.streetsblog.org/2017/09/21/the-campaign-to-fix-atlantas-most-dangerous-street-and-preserve-its-immigrant-cultures/.

"Transcript: Donald Trump Announces His Presidential Candidacy." *CBS News.* June 16, 2015, https://www.cbsnews.com/news/transcript-donald-trump-announces-his-presidential-candidacy/.

**Chapter One (Family)**

"2019 Demographics." *DC Health Matters.* January 2019, http://www.dchealthmatters.org/demographicdata?id=131494.

Hegedus, Amy, Ed.D. "Evaluating the Relationships Between Poverty and School Performance." *NWEA*, October 2018, https://www.nwea.org/resource-library/research/evaluating-the-relationships-between-poverty-and-school-performance-3.

Semuels, Alana. "Good School, Rich School; Bad School, Poor School." *The Atlantic*. August 25, 2016, https://www.theatlantic.com/business/archive/2016/08/property-taxes-and-unequal-schools/497333/.

## Chapter Two (Worthy)
None

## Chapter Three (Dreams)

Ducklow, Katie J. "Lessons for Social Workers: A Review of the Latino/a Undocumented Immigrant Experience." *Sophia*, the St. Catherine University Repository Website. 2017, https://sophia.stkate.edu/cgi/viewcontent.cgi?article=1726&context=msw_papers.

Holder, Sarah. "How Rule Changes About Public Benefits Could Affect Immigrants." *CityLab*. August 13, 2019, https://www.citylab.com/equity/2019/08/public-charge-rule-legal-immigration-welfare-services-dhs/595987/.

"States (and D.C.) That Allow Driver's Licenses for People in the Country Illegally," *Procon.Org*. December 20, 2019, https://immigration.procon.org/states-and-dc-that-allow-drivers-licenses-for-people-in-the-country-illegally/.

## Chapter Four (Friends)

Gonzalez, David. "In Today's Headlines, Echoes of Central America's Proxy Wars of the 1980s." *The New York Times*. February 27, 2019, https://www.nytimes.com/2019/02/27/lens/finding-echoes-of-to-days-headlines-in-central-americas-proxy-wars-in-the-1980s.html.

History.com Editors. "Hurricane Mitch." *History, A&E Television Networks*. Updated November 11, 2019, https://www.history.com/topics/natural-disasters-and-environment/hurricane-mitch.

*Lexico Dictionaries*. s.v. "proxy war." Accessed February 4, 2020, https://www.lexico.com/en/definition/proxy_war.

Rocha, Jose Luis, Thelma Martinez and Ximena Rocha. "Summing Up Hurricane Mitch: The Good, the Bad and the Ugly." *Envio*, December 1999, https://www.envio.org.ni/articulo/2289.

**Chapter Five (Life)**

"About Teen Pregnancy." *Division of Reproductive Health, National Center for Chronic Disease Prevention and Health Promotion*. March 1, 2019, https://www.cdc.gov/teenpregnancy/about/index.htm.

"'Drug Dealers, Criminals, Rapists': What Trump Thinks of Mexicans," *BBC News*, August 31, 2016, https://www.bbc.com/news/av/world-us-canada-37230916/drug-dealers-criminals-rapists-what-trump-thinks-of-mexicans.

"Trends in Teen Pregnancy and Childbearing." *Office of Population Affairs, U.S. Department of Health and Human Services*. Accessed January 23, 2020, https://www.hhs.gov/ash/oah/adolescent-development/reproductive-health-and-teen-pregnancy/teen-pregnancy-and-childbearing/trends/index.html.

Trump, Donald. *Twitter Post*. June 17, 2019, 9:20 PM, https://twitter.com/realdonaldtrump/status/1140791400658870274?lang=en.

## Chapter Six (Fear)

Israely, Jeff. "As the Global Economy Sinks, Tensions Over Immigration Rise." *Time*. February 6, 2009, http://content.time.com/time/world/article/0,8599,1876955,00.html.

"'It's All Done': President Donald Trump Teases Immigration Deal With Mexico NBC News." *NBC News*, YouTube. June 11, 2019, https://www.youtube.com/watch?v=stKWWZbvuc8.

Kauffman, Johnny. "Georgia Candidate for Governor Doesn't Plan to Use 'Deportation Bus' to Deport Anyone." *NPR*. May 16, 2018, https://www.npr.org/2018/05/16/611680288/georgia-candidate-for-governor-doesnt-plan-to-use-deportation-bus-to-deport-anyo.

Klinkner, Philip. "Op-Ed: Yes, Trump's Hard-Line Immigration Stance Helped Him Win the Election—But It Could Be His Undoing." *Los Angeles Times*. April 17, 2017, https://www.latimes.com/opinion/op-ed/la-oe-klinker-immigration-election-20170417-story.html.

McKee, Adam J. "Broken Windows Theory." *Encylopædia Britannica*. December 14, 2018, https://www.britannica.com/topic/broken-windows-theory.

Nowraseth, Alex. "Illegal Immigrants and Crime—Assessing the Evidence." *Cato Institute*. March 4, 2019, https://www.cato.org/blog/illegal-immigrants-crime-assessing-evidence.

"Selected Statistics on Farmworkers." *Farmworker Justice*. 2018, https://www.farmworkerjustice.org/sites/default/files/resources/NAWS%20data%20factsht%2010-18-18.pdf.

## Chapter Seven (Kinship)

Escobar, Natalie. "Family Separation Isn't New: U.S. Immigration Policy Has Traumatized Migrant Children and Parents for Nearly a Century." *The Atlantic.* August 14, 2018, https://www.theatlantic.com/family/archive/2018/08/us-immigration-policy-has-traumatized-children-for-nearly-100-years/567479/.

Greenfield, Victoria A., Blas Nuñez-Neto, Ian Mitch, Joseph C. Chang, and Etienne Rosas. "Human Smuggling and Associated Revenues: What Do or Can We Know About Routes from Central America to the United States?" *Homeland Security Operational Analysis Center. Rand Corporation.* 2019, https://www.rand.org/content/dam/rand/pubs/research_reports/RR2800/RR2852/RAND_RR2852.pdf

"Health Coverage of Immigrants." *The Henry J. Kaiser Family Foundation.* February 15, 2019, https://www.kff.org/disparities-policy/fact-sheet/health-coverage-of-immigrants/.

Lee, SungKyu and Jason Matejkowski. "Mental Health Service Utilization Among Noncitizens in the United States: Findings from the National Latino and Asian American Study." *Administration and Policy in Mental Health and Mental Health Services Research.* September 2012: 406-418, https://www.ncbi.nlm.nih.gov/pubmed/21755392.

Massey, Douglas S., Jorge Durand, and Karen A. Pren. "Why Border Enforcement Backfired." *The University of Chicago Press.* 2016: 1564, https://wws.princeton.edu/system/files/research/documents/684200.pdf.

Menjívar, Cecilia, and Andrea Gomez Cervantes. "El Salvador: Civil War, Natural Disasters, and Gang Violence Drive Migration." *Migration Policy Institute.* August 29, 2018, https://www.migrationpolicy.org/article/el-salvador-civil-war-natural-disasters-and-gang-violence-drive-migration.

*Merriam-Webster.com Dictionary.* s.v. "kin." Accessed January 31, 2020, https://www.merriam-webster.com/dictionary/kin.

*Merriam-Webster.com Dictionary.* s.v. "kinship." Accessed January 31, 2020, https://www.merriam-webster.com/dictionary/kinship.

## Chapter Eight (Acceptance)

Boyle, Gregory. *Tattoos on the Heart.* New York: Free Press, 2010.

Narayanan, Jayanth. "Diversity Is Good for Our Communities. Here's the Evidence." *World Economic Forum.* 2018, https://www.weforum.org/agenda/2018/04/people-who-live-in-diverse-neighbourhoods-are-more-helpful-here-s-how-we-know.

## Chapter Nine (Love)

Flynn, Mike, Shikha Dalmia, and Terry Colon. "What Part of Legal Immigration Don't You Understand?" *Reason Magazine.* October 2008, https://reason.org/wp-content/uploads/files/a87d1550853898a9b306ef458f116079.pdf.

Nowraseth, Alex. "1.3 Percent of All Central Americans in the Northern Triangle Were Apprehended by Border Patrol This Fiscal Year—So Far." *Cato Institute.* June 7, 2019, https://www.cato.org/blog/13-percent-all-central-americans-northern-triangle-were-apprehended-border-patrol-fiscal-year.

## Conclusion

Axelrod, Tal. "Trump Knocks Dems for Tweeting Obama-Era 'Kids in Cages' Photo," *The Hill.* July 11, 2019, https://thehill.com/homenews/administration/452575-trump-knocks-dems-for-tweeting-obama-era-kids-in-cages-photo.

Hains, Tim. "Obama DHS Sec. Jeh Johnson: I Freely Admit We Detained Children, 'It Was Necessary." *Real Clear Politics.* June 24, 2018, https://www.realclearpolitics.com/video/2018/06/24/obama_dhs_sec_jeh_johnson_we_detained_children_it_was_necessary.html.

"In Depth: Topics A to Z: Immigration." *Gallup.* 2020, https://news.gallup.com/poll/1660/immigration.aspx.

Valverde, Miriam. "Fact-checking Biden on Use of Cages for Immigrants During Obama Administration." *Politifact.* September 13, 2019, https://www.politifact.com/factchecks/2019/sep/13/joe-biden/fact-checking-biden-use-cages-during-obama-adminis/.

# ACKNOWLEDGEMENTS

———

A huge Thank You to all of the people that helped me create this book.

Paul, thank you for encouraging me in this project since before Day 1. I could not have done it without you. James, thank you for inspiring me to share my message through your love and zeal for life.

Thank you to my family and friends for all of your support and enthusiasm. It means so much to me.

Thank you to Eric Koester and the Creator Institute, Brian Bies, Leila Summers, Amanda Brown, Corey Whitbeck, and New Degree Press, and my editors Christine Smith, Alexander Pyles, and Linda Berardelli. Your help has been invaluable.

And thank you to everyone who: gave me their time for a personal interview, pre-ordered the eBook, paperback, and multiple copies to make publishing possible, helped spread the word about *Hola Miss* to gather amazing momentum, and helped me publish a book I am proud of. I am sincerely grateful for all of your help.

Karen Abron

James Abron

Haley Allen

Bridget Apap

Clara Apap

Ellie Apap

Jack Apap

John Apap

Maureen Apap

Teddy Apap

Tommy Apap

Peter Arkell

Bill and Joanne Arnette and Family

Cathi Athaide

Ken Athaide

Marie Athaide

Diego Azanza Rosillo

Daniel Barrett

Kinzer Barrett

Clayton Bassett

Joseph Benedetto

Audrey Rose Camp

Micaela Campbell

Wil Campbell

Prathyusha Chenji

Jack Collins

Matt Colvin

Camilla Comerford

Jim Comerford

James Comerford

Joey Comerford

Alden Corrigan

Charlie Corrigan

Delia Corrigan

Edward Corrigan

Frank Corrigan Jr.

Frank Corrigan III

Kevin Corrigan

Laura Corrigan

Lollie Corrigan

Louis Corrigan

Marie Corrigan

McLean Corrigan

Sam Corrigan

Vic Corrigan

Victor Corrigan III

William Costabile

Christopher Demetree

Margaret Demetree

Reina Demetree

Milton Diaz

Callum Feasey

Kristina Feasey

James Feasey

Chelsea Fetter

Hilary Fisher

Bill Fricke

Emma Fricke
Rose Fricke
Colin Gallagher
Kaitlin Gallagher
Sutton Gallagher
Montevia Gamble
Ella Garro
Evie Garro
Jeff Garro
Jessica Garro
Andrew Gould
Mary Clare Gould
Becky Grace
Terry Grace
Amelia Grace
Charlie Grace
Gabrielle Grace
Madeline Grace
Gene and Marylou
Habecker and Family
Justin Haight
Alexander Hegner
Chad Heiman
Sarah Heiman
Michael Hendricks
Nefi Hernández
Lauren Hogan
Vickie Hopkins and Family, and in memory of Buzz Hopkins
Grace Izard
Aveana Jackson

Maggie Johnson
Will Johnson
Colleen Jones
Eileen Jones
Elizabeth Jones
Matthew Jones
Tom Jones
Tommy Jones
Kelly King
Lee King
Parker King
Eric Koester
Matt and Amy Krengel and Family
Mark Krikorian
Melissa Lappe
Monica Laredo-Ruiz
Allison Link
Reilly Loflin
Charlie Loudermilk
Louise Loudermilk
Elizabeth MacGill
Marybeth Mangas
Byrne Marston
Douglas Massey
Mary Claire McClellan
Pat McNulty
Nicole McQueen
Katie Mitchell
Mary Murphy
Al and Kathie Napolitano and Family

Dave and Jean Napolitano
and Family
James Napolitano
Joe and Donna Napolitano
and Family
John Napolitano
Mark Napolitano
Mary Anne Napolitano
Paul Napolitano
Marvin Ochoa
Cherie Olivis
Leonard Olsen
Brandon Ona
Caroline O'Neal
Chris O'Neal
Natalia Ortega
Caitlyn Ownbey
Morgan Ownbey
Demetri Papademetrious
Marisa Parella
Kaitlin Picken
Marcos Pope
Jaclyn Proctor
Andrew Quigley
Maru Quigley
Francie Quigley
Chris Quigley
Angela Randazzo
Anthony Randazzo
Catherine Randazzo
Cathy Randazzo
Tony Randazzo

Balfre Rios
Rossany Rios
Robin Roberts
Tristan Roche
Juan Rodriguez
Cassandra Roman
Cynthia Roman
Benjamin Rossi
Samara Roth
Amanda Schaumann
Dan Schaumann
John Spalding
Mildred Spalding
Karen Sponselee
David Strange
Kevin Sullivan
Kortney Thurman
Jake Wamble
Katie Wamble
Janet Wells
Megan White
Joanna Williams
Steven Wilson
Diaon Woods
Bill Yarbrough
Lynne Yarbrough
Paul and Joelle Yarbrough
and Family
Anonymous

In memory of: Harry Apap, Claire Corrigan, Frank Corrigan Sr., Alfred Napolitano, and Victoria Napolitano.

Thank you to the people who modeled love and acceptance for me during their lifetimes: Paul Apap, Eileen Mosher Corrigan, and Billy Ray Smith.

To all the people and communities featured in my book: thank you for allowing me to have these experiences with you. Thank you especially to Grace House and the Grace House School-Based Mental Health team for accepting me and allowing me to grow through you.

Finally, thank you to my Grace House clients. Thank you for allowing me to learn about myself and God through knowing you.